THE LAW OF ALTERNATIVE DISPUTE RESOLUTION

2nd Edition

by
Margaret C. Jasper

Oceana's Legal Almanac Series
Law for the Layperson

2000
Oceana Publications, Inc.
Dobbs Ferry, New York

Information contained in this work has been obtained by Oceana Publications from sources believed to be reliable. However, neither the Publisher nor its authors guarantee the accuracy or completeness of any information published herein, and neither Oceana nor its authors shall be responsible for any errors, omissions or damages arising from the use of this information. This work is published with the understanding that Oceana and its authors are supplying information, but are not attempting to render legal or other professional services. If such services are required, the assistance of an appropriate professional should be sought.

Library of Congress Cataloging-in-Publication Data

Jasper, Margaret C.
  The law of dispute resolution : arbitration and alternative dispute resolution / by Margaret C. Jasper.—2nd ed.
      p. cm. — (Oceana's legal almanac series. Law for the layperson)
  Includes bibliographical references.
  ISBN 0-379-11343-0 (alk. paper)
    1. Dispute resolution (Law)—United States—Popular works.
    2. Arbitration and award—United States—Popular works.
    3. Compromise (Law)—United States—Popular works. I. Title. II. Series.

  KF9084.Z9 J37 2000
  347.73'9—dc21

                                                  00-57487

Oceana's Legal Almanac Series: Law for the Layperson
ISSN 1075-7376

©2000 by Oceana Publications, Inc.

To My Husband Chris

Your love and support
are my motivation and inspiration

-and-

In memory of my son, Jimmy

Table of Contents

CHAPTER 3:
MEDIATION

CHAPTER 4:
NEGOTIATION AND SETTLEMENT

CHAPTER 5:
COMMERCIAL DISPUTE RESOLUTION

CHAPTER 6:
EMPLOYMENT DISPUTE RESOLUTION

CHAPTER 7:
AUTOMOBILE INSURANCE CLAIM DISPUTE RESOLUTION

CHAPTER 8:
HEALTH CARE DISPUTE RESOLUTION

CHAPTER 9:
LABOR RELATIONS DISPUTE RESOLUTION

CHAPTER 10:
DIVORCE AND FAMILY RELATIONS DISPUTE RESOLUTION

APPENDICES

ABOUT THE AUTHOR

MARGARET C. JASPER is an attorney engaged in the general practice of law in South Salem, New York, concentrating in the areas of personal injury and entertainment law. Ms. Jasper holds a Juris Doctor degree from Pace University School of Law, White Plains, New York, is a member of the New York and Connecticut bars, and is certified to practice before the United States District Courts for the Southern and Eastern Districts of New York, and the United States Supreme Court. Ms. Jasper has been appointed to the panel of arbitrators of the American Arbitration Association and the law guardian panel for the Family Court of the State of New York, is a member of the Association of Trial Lawyers of America, and is a New York State licensed real estate broker and member of the Westchester County Board of Realtors, operating as Jasper Real Estate, in South Salem, New York.

Ms. Jasper is the author and general editor of the following legal almanacs: Juvenile Justice and Children's Law; Marriage and Divorce; Estate Planning; The Law of Contracts; The Law of Dispute Resolution; Law for the Small Business Owner; The Law of Personal Injury; Real Estate Law for the Homeowner and Broker; Everyday Legal Forms; Dictionary of Selected Legal Terms; The Law of Medical Malpractice; The Law of Product Liability; The Law of No-Fault Insurance; The Law of Immigration; The Law of Libel and Slander; The Law of Buying and Selling; Elder Law; The Right to Die; AIDS Law; The Law of Obscenity and Pornography; The Law of Child Custody; The Law of Debt Collection; Consumer Rights Law; Bankruptcy Law for the Individual Debtor; Victim's Rights Law; Animal Rights Law; Workers' Compensation Law; Employee Rights in the Workplace; Probate Law; Environmental Law; Labor Law; The Americans with Disabilities Act; The Law of Capital Punishment; Education Law; The Law of Violence Against Women; Landlord-Tenant Law; Insurance Law; Religion and the Law; Commercial Law; Motor Vehicle Law; Social Security Law; The Law of Drunk Driving; The Law of Speech and the First Amendment; Employment Discrimination Under Title VII; Hospital Liability Law; Home Mortgage Law Primer; Copyright Law; Patent Law; Trademark Law; and Special Education Law.

INTRODUCTION

Rarely does one go through life without encountering some kind of conflict or disagreement with another. Many of these conflicts become embroiled in the frustrating, costly and complex legal system, often taking numerous years to resolve with much uncertainty as to the outcome. Due in part to society's dissatisfaction with the present legal system, and the need for more expedient and less combative means for resolving problems, many have turned to alternative dispute resolution methods, such as arbitration, mediation and negotiation, to reach agreement on matters in conflict.

Recognizing that there is a need for such alternative dispute mechanisms, many programs have been instituted by both private organizations and government agencies, to provide dispute resolution services to those voluntarily wishing to avoid court. In addition, many federal and state statutes were enacted during the twentieth century, requiring that certain types of disputes be decided through arbitration and mediation procedures. Many courts have also began employing alternative dispute resolution methods for pending cases, in an effort to relieve the overcrowded court dockets.

This legal almanac explores the litigation process, and examines the alternative methods of dispute resolution presently available, and the areas in which they are used. It also explains the roles of the individuals who take part in these procedures, and the rules and guidelines which apply.

The Appendix provides sample documents, applicable statutes and other pertinent information and data. The Glossary contains definitions of many of the terms used throughout the almanac.

CHAPTER 1:
ALTERNATIVE DISPUTE RESOLUTION

IN GENERAL

Alternative dispute resolution (ADR) refers to the practice of resolving a disagreement to the satisfaction of all parties, in an expedient and economically feasible manner, rather than litigating the dispute. As reported by the American Arbitration Association (AAA), the world's leading provider of alternative dispute resolution services, mediation and arbitration are on this rise with a record-breaking 140,000 cases filed with the AAA in 1999. The 1999 filings represent a dramatic increase from the 95,143 cases filed with the AAA the previous year.

A variety of dispute resolution systems and techniques have been established to address a full range of business disputes involving, but not limited to, employment, consumer, technology, health care, bankruptcy, financial services, accounting, international trade and mass claims. Mass tort claims have arisen in the areas of products liability, and include claims relating to tobacco, asbestos, Dalkon Shield, heart valves and silicone breast implants. ADR has also been used to help resolve conflicts in the energy industry as well as the resolution of environmental issues. Mediation also plays a very big role in resolving personal conflicts, such as those which may occur in the context of divorce and custody lawsuits.

A national directory of organizations offering dispute resolution services is set forth at Appendix 1 and a directory of international arbitration organizations is set forth at Appendix 2.

ALTERNATIVE TO LITIGATION

The term alternative dispute resolution infers that there is already a standard dispute resolution procedure in place. Litigation is the most formal, and the most time-consuming of the dispute resolution methods. Litigation is complicated, costly, and can go on for years. Alternative dispute resolution allows for a more expedient resolution of a conflict and is more likely to preserve the relationship among the parties to the dispute because it reduces the enormous stress and resentment litigation necessarily creates. Alternative dispute resolution also affords the parties complete confidentiality, unlike court records which are open to the public, and also enables the parties to choose their fact finder.

In order to better understand alternative dispute resolution, one must first understand the process of litigation.

Adversarial vs. Inquisitorial Systems

Litigation in the United States is an adversarial procedure, which relies on the presumably neutral and impartial judgment of the factfinder—the judge or jury—based on the facts and applicable law. The parties to the litigation are each responsible for developing their own legal theory, and providing their evidence, in order to prove their case and prevail in the dispute. The judge or jury considers all of the evidence and arguments set forth by the parties. Once the parties have set forth their case, the judge or jury is entrusted to make the final decision, which is a court order the parties are legally bound to obey or risk facing a contempt citation.

Unlike the American system, many international legal systems are founded upon the inquisitorial system of justice. Generally, the inquisitorial system employs specially trained judges to both investigate the facts of the dispute, and make the final decision. The parties to the litigation are not responsible for setting forth their case as they do in the adversarial system. Their role is basically to respond to any questions set forth by the judges.

The Evolution of the American Legal System

Following the Revolutionary War, the states drafted constitutions which provided for three branches of state government: the legislative, executive and judicial branches. The judicial branch borrowed heavily from the English legal system. Courts were organized in a hierarchy ranging from the lowest level of court with limited jurisdiction to the highest appellate court, which reviews decisions of the lower courts at its discretion.

The federal constitution was modeled after the New York State constitution, and created the same three branches of government as did the states. The first federal court to be established was the United States Supreme Court. The federal court system has evolved to include federal district courts in each state, and a system of federal appellate courts. There are also federal courts which govern specific areas of the law, such as tax and bankruptcy matters.

The United States Supreme Court is the highest appellate court in the federal system. It also retains original jurisdiction over certain limited matters, such as disputes involving constitutional issues or matters involving a federal law. Its appellate review of decisions are heard at the court's discretion, and review of state court decisions depends on whether the state court wrongly applied federal law.

The Litigation Process

A litigated dispute begins with the filing of a lawsuit by one of the parties to the dispute. This is accomplished by service of a summons and complaint upon the other party. Service is undertaken by a person authorized by law to serve legal documents, such as the sheriff or a process server. Many jurisdictions also permit a non-party, over the age of 18, to serve legal documents.

Depending on the jurisdiction, the party bringing the lawsuit is known as the plaintiff or petitioner, and the party against whom the lawsuit is filed is known as the defendant or respondent. The complaint details the plaintiff's claim against the defendant, and sets forth the legal theory under which the plaintiff seeks to prevail. The lawsuit must be filed within the statutorily prescribed period of time for the particular type of action. This time period is referred to as the statute of limitations.

Upon receipt of the summons and complaint, the defendant must respond to the complaint within a prescribed period of time or risk losing the dispute by default. The defendant may serve an answer to the complaint, or may choose to make a motion seeking to dismiss the complaint prior to serving his or her answer. If the motion is granted, the case is dismissed. However, if the motion is denied, the defendant must serve an answer within a statutorily defined time period following the decision on the motion.

The defendant's answer admits or denies the allegations set forth in the complaint, and presents any defenses to the allegations that the defendant may have. Additionally, if the defendant has his or her own claims against the plaintiff, known as counterclaims, these allegations are also set forth in the defendant's answer. The plaintiff is then required to serve an answer addressing the counterclaim.

The litigation procedure, from initiation of the lawsuit to final disposition, is governed by the statutory law of the particular court in which the lawsuit is filed. During the pendency of the lawsuit, much of litigation is accomplished on paper. There are numerous motions which a party may file and ask the assigned judge to rule upon. A motion, which may be made orally or in writing, is an application to the court requesting an order or a ruling in favor of the applicant.

For example, a party may make a motion seeking some type of interim relief, such as the production of certain evidence. The notice of motion and any supporting papers are served upon the other party, who usually responds in opposition to the motion. Thus, motion practice is in itself a series of adversarial procedures, because the substance of the motion is disputed by the litigants or their attorneys, either by written arguments or orally before the judge.

Litigation usually involves a lengthy discovery process. Typical discovery may include the exchange of detailed information, the examination of documents and other evidence, and an oral examination of the parties and prospective witnesses in a proceeding known as a deposition or examination before trial, depending on the jurisdiction.

During a deposition, the deponent is placed under oath, and must answer a series of questions put forth by the parties or their attorneys. The sworn testimony given at the deposition is recorded by a legal stenographer, who prepares a transcript of the depositions for use at trial. The deposition testimony pins down each deponent's version of the facts, and can be used to impeach a party or non-party witness.

As the lawsuit nears trial, the judge will usually set the matter down for a settlement conference, in an attempt to resolve the dispute without going to trial. Absent a successful outcome, the lawsuit eventually goes to trial, after which a decision is rendered by the judge or jury. The parties may seek to appeal unfavorable decisions to higher courts. Once the appeals process has been exhausted, the decision is final and enforceable. In addition, the decision serves to set a precedent for that particular type of dispute, which must generally be adhered to by the same and lower-level courts of the same jurisdiction, in similar disputes.

THE AMERICAN ARBITRATION ASSOCIATION

The American Arbitration Association ("AAA") was founded in 1926 to provide a forum for the resolution of a wide range of disputes through mediation, arbitration, elections and other out-of-court settlement techniques. The AAA is a not-for-profit public service organization with 38 offices in the United States, and operating under 53 cooperative agreements with arbitral institutions in 38 countries.

A national directory of American Arbitration Association (AAA) offices is set forth at Appendix 3.

The AAA maintains a roster of nearly 17,000 impartial experts—known as neutrals—who hear and resolve cases. Neutrals are nominated to the AAA's National Roster of Arbitrators and Mediators by leaders in their industry or profession. These neutrals are recognized for their standing and expertise in their fields, and their integrity and dispute resolution skills.

Roster candidates are screened using an intensive, two-tiered process which evaluates management skills, substantive expertise, commitment, ethics, training and suitability to the regional caseload. Qualifications include a minimum of ten (10) years of senior level business experience or legal practice, honors and awards indicating leadership in their field, and training and experience in arbitration or other forms of dispute resolution.

The AAA provides education and training for those involved in dispute resolution as neutrals and advocates, and monitors and evaluates their performance on an ongoing basis. The conduct of arbitrators is guided by the AAA's Code of Ethics, prepared by a Joint Committee of the American Arbitration Association and the American Bar Association.

The Code of Ethics for Arbitrators in commercial disputes is set forth at Appendix 4.

The conduct of mediators is governed by the Model Standards of Conduct for Mediators, developed by the American Arbitration Association, the American Bar Association and the Society of Professionals in Dispute Resolution.

The Model Standards of Conduct for Mediators is set forth at Appendix 5.

FEDERAL DISPUTE RESOLUTION

In 1990, Congress passed the Administrative Dispute Resolution Act (ADRA), which was subsequently revised in 1996. Under the ADRA, Congress mandated that federal agencies create internal alternative dispute resolution programs, and use alternative dispute resolution methods, to resolve disputes in the federal sector. Although the use of alternative dispute resolution methods has increased dramatically, resolving disputes in the federal sector can be problematic because, unlike traditional private sector dispute resolution, the ADRA contains many restrictions that govern its use in the public sector.

In order to assist federal agencies in developing and administering ADR programs, the AAA created the Federal Center for Dispute Resolution to meet the growing dispute resolution needs of the public sector. The AAA provides a list of mediators with extensive federal sector experience and impressive credentials from every geographic region of the country.

The text of the Administrative Dispute Resolution Act is set forth at Appendix 6.

TRENDS IN ALTERNATIVE DISPUTE RESOLUTION

There are various methods of alternative dispute resolution, with differing degrees of formality. The primary methods of alternative dispute resolution include arbitration, mediation, and negotiation, which are explored in more detail in the following chapters.

As set forth below, less formal methods of dispute resolution—such as private trials, summary jury trials, and mini-trials—are also emerging as viable ADR mechanisms to support the systems already in place.

The Private Trial

Some states have statutes which permit the parties to a dispute to select and hire a referee to preside over the case in a privately-held trial. This procedure is commonly referred to as "Rent-A-Judge." In general, the parties to the dispute must petition the court in which the case has been filed for permission to hire their own judge—usually an individual familiar with the law and procedural rules of the jurisdiction, such as a retired judge. If the court grants the petition, the case is transferred to the hired judge.

The hired judge hears the case, and issues a decision, which is transmitted to the original judge and converted into an enforceable order. Parties who oppose the findings of the hired judge are permitted to appeal the decision in the same manner as if the decision had been made by the original judge following trial. Although the parties must pay the hired judge, the procedure offers important advantages over litigation.

For example, the litigants are able to have their dispute resolved expeditiously instead of waiting for the original judge to place the matter on his or her trial calendar. In addition, the parties have the opportunity to hire a judge who is particularly knowledgeable about the subject matter of the dispute.

Summary Jury Trial

A summary jury trial is a procedure whereby the parties to a lawsuit are permitted to present a shortened version of their case before a group of prospective jurors, known as an advisory jury. The non-binding verdict rendered by the advisory jury serves as a guide to the litigants of the possible outcome of a full-blown jury trial. Additionally, the attorneys for the litigants are permitted to question the advisory jury members concerning their view of the case. It is expected that this information will compel the litigants to seriously negotiate a settlement of the dispute. If the subsequent negotiations are unsuccessful, the parties may resume prosecuting their case before a different judge and jury.

Mini-Trial

The mini-trial is similar to the summary jury trial in that the mini-trial also presents a shortened version of the dispute. Instead of a jury, the mini-trial is held before a neutral advisor who has been hired by the parties. The neutral advisor plays whatever role in the process that the parties desire. The neutral advisor's role may change during the process, depending on the success of post-trial settlement negotiations. The neutral advisor may start out as a mediator, and ultimately be asked to arbitrate the dispute if an impasse is reached in the negotiations.

The lawyer for each litigant presents the case under certain prescribed guidelines designed to expedite the process. There is no record made of the proceedings. Witnesses may be called, however, given the time constraints, it is more likely that a summary of the deposition testimony of the witness will be admitted instead. Final arguments are conducted within in an agreed upon time limit.

After the case has been presented, the neutral advisor and the parties meet to discuss the possibility of settlement. Because the parties have had the benefit of hearing a preview of the actual trial, they are better able to judge the merits and risks of their case.

The mini-trial offers many advantages. The proceedings are expedient, confidential, flexible and informal. The rules of evidence are not strictly applied. The cost of a mini-trial is estimated as one-tenth of the cost of litigating the same dispute.

CHAPTER 2:
ARBITRATION

IN GENERAL

Arbitration is the process whereby an impartial third party, known as an arbitrator, listens to both sides of the dispute and issues a binding decision. Arbitration is similar to—but less formal than—a trial before a judge. Arbitration of a matter may come about in several ways. For example, the agreement to arbitrate a dispute may be entirely voluntary, or may be court-ordered. Specific matters, such as disputes involving management-labor disputes, are subject to arbitration according to statute.

The federal government, as well as many of the states, has enacted statutes relating to arbitration in certain instances.

The text of the Federal Arbitration Act is set forth at Appendix 7 and a chart of federal and state arbitration statutes is set forth at Appendix 8.

In 1955, the Conference of Commissioners on Uniform State Laws designed the Uniform Arbitration Act, which has served as a model for many state arbitration statutes.

The text of the Uniform Arbitration Act is set forth at Appendix 9.

SUBMITTING A DISPUTE TO ARBITRATION

In most cases, the decision to arbitrate a dispute is entirely voluntary, however, as further discussed below, some of these techniques are utilized by the present court system in an effort to reduce costs, avoid trial and streamline the litigation process.

Voluntary arbitration is most commonly used to decide contract disputes, however, the arbitration process is being looked upon as a valuable means to resolve disputes arising in many other areas, including consumer disputes, copyright, trademark and patent infringement disputes, and insurance matters.

Voluntary arbitration differs from litigation in many important aspects. For example, the parties are free to select their finder of fact in an arbitration hearing, whereas a judge or jury serves as the factfinder in a trial. Arbitration also offers privacy to the parties whereas litigation is generally open to the public. In addition, although the parties surrender control over the outcome of the dispute to the arbitrator, they are free to set forth the procedures and standards by which the arbitrator resolves the matter.

For example, the parties may agree that the arbitrator's award will be merely advisory and non-binding, or they may determine that the award will be binding and enforceable in a court of law. The parties may set forth the procedural details, such as the timing and method of introducing evidence, and the manner in which witnesses may be produced.

Arbitration offers many advantages over litigation. Arbitration is less costly, and disputes are generally resolved in much less time than when they are submitted to the court. Court calendars are backlogged and litigants may wait months or years to have their day in court. In the meantime, the escalating expense of litigation is in many cases prohibitive.

The cost of arbitration is comparatively low, and is more predictable, than litigation. Generally, the parties pay a filing fee, an administration fee, and the arbitrator's fee. However, if the arbitration hearing should be prolonged, the arbitrator's fee can become substantial—and the loser may have to pay all of the expenses of the arbitration hearing.

Nevertheless, there are other disadvantages which may deter some parties from submitting their dispute to arbitration. As discussed below, discovery rights are limited. This means that if a party wishes to hide important information, they will likely succeed. In addition, the parties generally do not have the right to appeal the arbitrator's decision as they would be entitled to do following a judicial decision.

Therefore, if you are leaning towards including an arbitration clause in an agreement, but are concerned about some of the disadvantages which accompany arbitration, you should attempt to detail the arbitration procedure as fully as possible in the arbitration clause, should the subject matter of the agreement end up in controversy.

Arbitration of a dispute usually occurs in one of two ways:

> (1) By Demand—The parties to a contract provide in the contract that arbitration would be the means of resolving any disputes that may arise during performance of that contract. When a dispute arises under the contract, one of the parties may file a Demand for Arbitration pursuant to the arbitration clause.

A sample contract arbitration clause is set forth at Appendix 10 and a Demand for Arbitration form is set forth at Appendix 11.

(2) By Submission—The parties to an existing dispute agree to resolve the controversy through the process of arbitration.

A sample agreement to submit a dispute to arbitration is set forth at Appendix 12 and the AAA submission form is set forth at Appendix 13.

The parties may choose to utilize the Commercial Arbitration Rules set forth by the American Arbitration Association as the governing standard for the process.

The AAA Commercial Arbitration Rules are set forth at Appendix 14.

PROCEDURAL STEPS

If the parties decide to use the services of the American Arbitration Association, there are procedural steps which must be followed in order to initiate the arbitration procedure. The exact steps may differ slightly depending on whether the arbitration was initiated by demand or by submission.

Once a matter has been submitted for arbitration, an arbitrator will be chosen and the process will begin. Usually, the arbitrator will meet with the parties and/or their attorneys, to discuss the issues and set up a discovery schedule.

The arbitration hearing generally begins with opening statements, much like a trial. Each party, or their attorney, will briefly state their positions, what their case will prove, and the outcome to which they believe they are entitled. The claimant will then present its case by producing evidence, such as witnesses or documentation. The respondent is entitled to cross-examine any witnesses produced by the claimant. After the claimant rests his or her case, the respondent will present its case in the same manner as did the claimant, and the claimant will also be permitted the right to cross-examine the respondent's witnesses, if any.

The last stage of the arbitration hearing is the final argument, made by the parties or their attorneys, by which the party attempts to undermine his or her opponent's case and promote its own case. Each party emphasizes his or her evidence, and the rationale he or she believes should prevail. The arbitrator then closes the hearing and renders a final and binding decision sometime thereafter, which is enforceable in a court of law.

Although the arbitration hearing appears to parallel a trial, the parties to the arbitration hearing do forego certain rights they would have had in a trial, in order to expedite the arbitration process. For example, the rules of evidence are relaxed in arbitration, making it quite easy to enter into evidence items which would never be permitted at trial. In addition, access to pre-trial discovery is limited whereas in litigation, there is a trend towards allowing full and extensive discovery of the opponent's case.

SUBPOENAS IN THE ARBITRATION PROCESS

Anyone authorized by law to issue subpoenas may do so in arbitration in order to subpoena witnesses or documents. In addition, under many arbitration statutes, the arbitrator can issue subpoenas either at the request of a party or independently. In either instance, the parties are responsible for preparation of the subpoena service and enforcement. Where there is a panel of three arbitrators, unless the law provides to the contrary, or the parties otherwise agree, decisions on subpoena issuance should be made by a majority of the panel.

Procedure

The following steps generally take place when subpoenas are sought by a party in a AAA arbitration proceeding:

1. The party or attorney informs the AAA case administrator of its wish to request a subpoena.

2. The AAA case administrator sends the subpoena form to the party or attorney for completion.

3. The party or attorney completes the subpoena form and returns it to the administrator.

4. The administrator sends the completed subpoena form to the arbitrator for review and signature, if determined by the arbitrator to be appropriate. In some instances, an arbitrator may question the need for the subpoena requested and ask the case administrator to obtain detailed information from the requesting party to aid the arbitrator in deciding whether or not to sign the subpoena. If the arbitrator deems it appropriate, the subpoena request my be disclosed to all parties. In the alternative, the arbitrator might reserve decision, subject to oral argument of the parties at the time of the hearing.

5. If acceptable, the arbitrator signs the subpoena and returns it to the administrator. If time is of the essence, the arbitrator, with the approval of the administrator, may forward the signed subpoena directly to the requesting party or attorney.

6. The administrator receives the subpoena and returns it to the requesting party or attorney.

7. The requesting party or attorney serves the subpoena on the witness or custodian of documents.

Copies of correspondence or other information with respect to subpoenas are normally not exchanged between the parties or discussed. By mutual agreement of the parties or at the direction of the arbitrator, however, copies of such correspondence and subpoenas may be exchanged between the parties.

A party to the arbitration who is served with a subpoena and questions the authority of the arbitrator, may raise the issue before the arbitrator at the hearing. The arbitrator may then rule as to whether the subpoena should be quashed. However, if a subpoena is simply ignored, it is up to the requesting party to have that subpoena enforced through a court of proper jurisdiction. In addition, arbitrators may draw "negative inferences" about a party's failure to abide by a subpoena.

Out-of-State Witnesses

Under certain circumstances, an individual located out-of-state can be subpoenaed. However, this requires review of the applicable law under the particular circumstances Ultimately, enforcement of the subpoena lies with the court, not the arbitrator.

COURT-ANNEXED ARBITRATION

Many state and federal courts have begun to employ arbitration as a means to relieve the number of cases placed on the burgeoning trial calendars, and reduce the enormous cost that litigation places on the system. In general, the process involves the diversion of certain qualified cases from the litigation track to a court-supervised arbitration process. A court-certified arbitrator, or panel of arbitrators, is appointed by the court, or alternatively chosen by the parties, to preside over the arbitration hearing.

The arbitrator hears the dispute and examines the evidence. As in private arbitration, the procedural and evidentiary rules are not as strictly adhered to as in a formal trial. The arbitrator renders a decision by determining the facts and applying the law of the jurisdiction in which the case is pending. This distinguishes court assigned arbitration from private arbitration wherein the parties are free to choose the governing standards used to resolve the dispute. The parties review the arbitrator's decision and, if they are in agreement, the arbitrator's ruling may be converted into an enforceable court order by the judge originally assigned to the matter. If the parties disagree with the ruling, they may, depending on the jurisdiction and the circumstances, request a trial.

THE ARBITRATOR

The parties to arbitration are permitted to choose the arbitrator, who usually has expertise in the particular area of dispute. In some instances, the parties will each choose one arbitrator and they, in turn, will choose an additional third arbitrator to create a panel who will decide the case. In choosing an arbitrator, it is important to review his or her credentials, particularly in the subject matter of the dispute. One may obtain referrals from friends and business associates who have successfully used arbitration.

Arbitrator Disclosure

Because the arbitrator is required to be neutral and independent, ascertain whether there is any existing conflict of interest which would prevent the arbitrator from exercising independent judgment of the dispute. The AAA's rules require that neutral arbitrators be impartial, and that the parties have confidence in their impartiality.

Under AAA rules, arbitrators must disclose any relationship between themselves and a party, a party's representative, or a witness. The rules require every neutral arbitrator "to disclose to the AAA any circumstances likely to affect his or her impartiality, including any bias or any financial or personal interest in the result of the arbitration or any past or present relationship with the parties or their representatives." This is also dealt with in detail in the Code of Ethics for Commercial Arbitrators.

To facilitate disclosure by arbitrators, the AAA has adopted a Notice of Appointment form which must be executed by every neutral arbitrator in every case at the time of appointment. The arbitrator must indicate on this form whether or not there is a disclosure to be made.

Every disclosure, no matter how insignificant should be communicated to the parties. If information received from the arbitrator or another source seems vague or incomplete, further inquiries should be made to gather pertinent facts for transmittal to the parties. When making a disclosure the arbitrator should provide the following information regarding the relationship that is being disclosed:

1. Whether the relationship is in the past, present, or anticipated in the future;

2. The nature of the relationship;

3. The duration of relationship (from when to when)

4. Whether business is being conducted directly or indirectly;

5. Whether the disclosed relationship is professional, social or familial;

6. The extent of contact—daily, weekly, monthly, yearly;

7. The contact event (e.g., business meetings; occupying space in the same building; consultation; legal professional representation; professional or trade association meeting or committee work; intimate social gathering; large group social gathering; etc.);

8. Whether the relationships affect the arbitrator's ability to act impartially.

Although the major burden of disclosure falls on the arbitrator, responsibility to ascertain potentially disqualifying facts also rests on the parties.

After an arbitrator makes a disclosure, the parties are notified about the disclosure, in writing, by the Case Administrator, and given a specific time period within which to comment on the arbitrator's disclosure. If both parties agree that the arbitrator should be removed, the Association will so notify the arbitrator, and a replacement arbitrator may be appointed.

If the parties don't agree to remove the arbitrator, the AAA will review the parties' written contentions regarding the reaffirmation or removal of the arbitrator, and will make a determination which is final and binding. The rules provide conclusive administrative authority with the AAA, subject always to court review in contested situations, to rule on the arbitrator's qualifications to serve in a given case.

If an arbitrator, at any time, discloses a degree of bias that clearly violates the requirement of impartiality, the AAA may arrange for the replacement of the arbitrator, after consultation with the parties.

Arbitrators are generally not advised by the AAA when their service has been challenged. In the event the AAA must seek further clarification from the arbitrator regarding a disclosure, they do so without making reference to any particular party.

If the arbitrator fails to make a disclosure, a final award may be vacated depending on the circumstances. For example, the following circumstances were deemed sufficient by the courts to require vacatur of the award on the ground of partiality:

1. Present or recent attorney-client relationship;

2. Relationship of consanguinity within six degrees (e.g. second cousins);

3. Business dealings which are significant, ongoing, or regularly conducted;

4. Close social relations or friendships;

5. Arbitrator had a case in which the arbitrator was a party or counsel before one who is now a party or counsel.

Code of Ethics for Arbitrators in Commercial Disputes

The Code of Ethics for Arbitrators in Commercial Disputes was prepared in 1977 by a joint committee consisting of a special committee of the American Arbitration Association and a special committee of the American Bar Association. It has been approved and recommended by both organizations.

Persons who act as commercial arbitrators undertake serious responsibilities to the public as well as to the parties involved in the proceeding. Those responsibilities include important ethical obligations. Although few cases of unethical behavior by commercial arbitrators have arisen, the American Bar Association and the American Arbitration Association believe that it is in the public interest to set forth generally accepted standards of ethical conduct for guidance of arbitrators and parties in commercial disputes.

This Code is intended to apply to all proceedings in which disputes or claims are submitted for decision to one or more arbitrators appointed in a manner provided by an agreement of the parties, by applicable arbitration rules, or by law. In all such cases, the persons who have the power to decide should observe fundamental standards of ethical conduct. In the Code, all such persons are called "arbitrators" although, in some types of cases, they might be called "umpires" or have some other title.

Various aspects of the conduct of arbitrators, including some matters covered by this Code, may be governed by agreement of the parties, by arbitration rules to which the parties have agreed, or by applicable law. This Code does not take the place of or supersede such agreements, rules, or laws and does not establish new or additional grounds for judicial review of arbitration awards.

While this Code is intended to provide ethical guidelines in many types of arbitration, it does not form a part of the arbitration rules of the American Arbitration Association or of any other organization, nor is it intended to apply to mediation or conciliation. In addition, labor arbitration is governed by the Code of Professional Responsibility for Arbitrators of Labor-Management Disputes, not by this Code.

In some types of arbitration, there are three or more arbitrators. In such cases, it is sometimes the practice for each party, acting alone, to appoint one arbitrator and for the other arbitrators to be designated by those two, by the parties, or by an independent institution or individual. The sponsors of this Code believe that it is preferable for parties to agree that all arbitrators should comply with the same ethical standards. However, it is recognized that there is a long-established practice in some types of arbitration for the arbitrators who are appointed by one party, acting alone, to be governed by special ethical considerations. Those special considerations are set forth in the last section of the Code, headed "Ethical Considerations Relating to Arbitrators Appointed by One Party."

Although this Code is sponsored by the American Arbitration Association and the American Bar Association, its use is not limited to arbitrations administered by the AAA or to cases in which the arbitrators are lawyers. Rather, it is presented as a public service to provide guidance in all types of commercial arbitration.

The Code of Ethics for Arbitrators in Commercial Disputes is set forth at Appendix 4.

Requirements for AAA National Roster of Arbitrators

Applicants for membership on the AAA National Roster of Arbitrators and Mediators must meet or exceed the following requirements:

Qualifications

1. Minimum of 10 years of senior-level business or professional experience or legal practice;

2. Educational degree(s) and/or professional license(s) appropriate to their field of expertise;

3. Honors, awards and citations indicating leadership in their field;

4. Training and experience in arbitration and/or other forms of dispute resolution;

5. Membership in a professional association(s); and

6. Other relevant experience or accomplishments (e.g. published articles).

Neutrality

1. Freedom from bias or prejudice; and

2. The ability to evaluate and apply legal, business or trade principles.

Judicial Capacity

1. The ability to manage the hearing process; and

2. The ability to make a thorough and impartial evaluation of testimony and other evidence.

Reputation

1. Must be held in the highest regard by peers for integrity, fairness and good judgement; and

2. Dedicated to upholding the AAA Code of Ethics for Arbitrators and/or Standards of Conduct for Mediators.

Commitment to ADR Process

The applicant must exhibit a willingness to devote time and effort when selected to serve.

Letters of Recommendation

The applicant must furnish letters from at least four active professionals in the applicant's field, but not from any firms or professional associations in which the applicant is employed or on which the applicant currently serves as an officer, director or trustee. Each letter must address the following:

1. Nature and duration of the relationship; and

2. Why the applicant would be qualified to serve.

The AAA suggests the following sources for recommendation letters:

1. A current AAA Panel Member;

2. A current or former state or federal judge;

3. An attorney who served as the applicant's opposing counsel; or

4. A former employer or client.

Personal Letter

The applicant must submit a letter explaining why the applicant feels he or she would like to be included on AAA's Roster of Arbitrators and Mediators and to what extent the applicant will commit to serving and representing the AAA. The applicant should also indicate in the letter whether or not they are currently serving as a neutral with any other ADR agencies.

AAA Training for Commercial Arbitrators

The AAA has a Commercial Arbitrator Development Program that provides nationally-standardized education and training for all commercial arbitrators on their National Roster of Neutrals. The overall key components of the Program are:

1. Initial training in the fundamentals of the arbitration process;

2. Advanced training in case management techniques;

3. An annual arbitrator update requirement; and

4. An annual continuing education requirement.

Arbitrator Development Path for Commercial Arbitrators Joining on or after January 1, 2000.

As of January 1, 2000, everyone recruited to the AAA's National Roster of Commercial Arbitrators was required to successfully complete approximately 28 hours of education and training their first year, 20 hours their second year, and a minimum of 8 hours every year thereafter.

Within six months of their Roster admission date, arbitrators joining the Roster on or after January 1, 2000 are required to successfully complete the Arbitrator I Training Course subtitled *Fundamentals of the Arbitration Process: An Introduction to Case Management Techniques*. This 24-hour course consists of 8 hours of home study plus 16 hours of classroom participation in a workshop setting.

Within the second year of their initial appointment to the Roster, arbitrators joining the Roster on or after January 1, 2000 are required to successfully complete the Arbitrator II Training Course subtitled *Advanced Case Management Techniques*. This 16-hour practicum covers, in greater detail and more intensely, the various case management techniques addressed in the Arbitrator I Training.

Beginning with their second year, and every year thereafter for as long as they remain on the Roster, arbitrators joining the Roster on or after January 1, 2000 are required to successfully complete a 4-hour program covering changes in AAA rules and procedures, legal updates concerning significant court decisions and relevant revisions to state and federal laws affecting arbitration.

Beginning with their third year, and every year thereafter for as long as they remain on the Roster, arbitrators joining the Roster on or after January 1, 2000 are required to successfully complete a minimum of 4 hours of Arbitrator Continuing Education (ACE). This is in addition to the 4-hour Annual Arbitrator Update.

Arbitrator Development Path for Current Commercial Arbitrators.

The requirements of the Arbitrator Development Path for Current Commercial Arbitrators are the successful completion of at least 6 hours of initial training, 16 hours of advanced training and, eventually, a minimum of 8 hours of continuing education every year. These requirements apply to all commercial arbitrators who were on the Association's National Roster before November 1, 1999.

The successful completion of The Commercial Arbitrator Workshop is mandatory for all commercial arbitrators, excluding construction panelists, on the panel prior to January 1, 2000 regardless of prior training or experience. After attending this workshop, commercial arbitrators will next be required to attend the Arbitrator II advanced training described below.

After completing the Commercial Arbitrator Training Workshop, arbitrators subject to the Arbitrator Development Path for Current Commercial Arbitrators will be required to successfully complete the Arbitrator Training II course subtitled *Advanced Case Management Techniques*. This 16-hour practicum covers, in greater detail and more intensely, the various case management techniques addressed in the two fundamental workshops.

At a date yet to be determined, a minimum of four (4) hours of annual Arbitrator Continuing Education will become mandatory for all arbitrators subject to the Arbitrator Development Path for Current Commercial Arbitrators.

CHAPTER 3:
MEDIATION

IN GENERAL

Mediation is a less formal method of alternative dispute resolution than arbitration. Mediation, like arbitration, enlists the assistance of a neutral third party, known as a mediator. However, the role of the mediator differs from that of the arbitrator. The mediator does not issue a binding decision but rather assists the opposing parties in resolving their own dispute, which resolution may then be formalized in a written agreement. The mediator cannot force the parties to change their positions. Thus, the parties remain responsible for negotiating a settlement of their dispute.

Mediation is particularly attractive to those persons who like to exercise control over the outcome of their disputes. It is a private and confidential procedure; and it is voluntary and freely terminable, unless statutorily prescribed or court-ordered. Nevertheless, for mediation to be successful, the parties who agree to mediate their dispute must do so with a cooperative spirit and a good faith willingness to mediate.

Mediation is being used to resolve disputes arising in many areas, including matters involving domestic relations, contracts, securities, consumer complaints, construction claims, and labor-management relations.

ADVANTAGES OF MEDIATION

Mediation provides many advantages over litigation, as follows:

1. The parties are directly engaged in the negotiation of the settlement.

2. The mediator, as a neutral third party, can view the dispute objectively and can assist the parties in exploring alternatives which they might not have considered on their own.

3. As mediation can be scheduled at an early stage in the dispute, a settlement can be reached much more quickly than in litigation.

4. Parties generally save money through reduced legal costs and less staff time.

5. Mediators have been carefully chosen for their knowledge and experience. Attorneys and nonattorneys from many professions, all of whom have received extensive training, serve on the AAA's roster of mediators.

6. Parties enhance the likelihood of continuing their business relationship

7. Creative solutions or accommodations to special needs of the parties can become a part of the settlement.

8. Information disclosed at a mediation may not be divulged as evidence in any arbitral, judicial or other proceeding.

THE MEDIATION PROCEDURE

Parties may choose to adopt mediation as part of their contractual dispute settlement procedure by including a mediation clause in their contract in conjunction with the arbitration clause.

A sample contract mediation clause is set forth at Appendix 15 and a Request for Mediation is set forth at Appendix 16.

Where there is no contractual provision, the parties can agree to submit their dispute to mediation. If a matter is already pending in court, by agreement of the litigating parties or the court, a mediation may proceed.

A sample agreement to mediate a dispute is set forth at Appendix 17.

The parties choose a mediator and meet with the mediator to discuss the issues of the dispute. Each side is given the opportunity to express their position. The mediator explains the mediation procedure to the parties and answers any questions they may have.

Following the initial meeting, the mediator generally meets individually with each of the parties so that they can express their positions clearly and openly. During 'the individual sessions, the mediator presents and discusses each party's concerns with the other party, in an effort to reach some common ground.

After meeting with each party individually, the mediator may schedule another joint session with all parties present, to determine whether they are progressing. The process of meeting individually and jointly continues until a settlement is obtained—if possible—in which case the mediator will assist the parties in formalizing their written agreement.

Most mediation cases are settled in a few hours. Others may require additional time, depending on the complexity of the issues. According to the AAA, national statistics indicate that 85% of commercial matters and 95%

of personal injury matters end in written settlement agreements. Although mediation itself is not binding, a signed settlement agreement is as enforceable as any other contractual agreement. A properly executed agreement may be used in litigation should one of the parties breach the terms of the agreement.

If the mediation is unsuccessful, the case may proceed to arbitration. In that case, any mediation fee paid to the AAA will be applied towards the arbitration fee provided that the arbitration case is filed with the AAA within 90 days of the termination of the mediation.

CHOOSING A MEDIATOR

Choosing the right mediator for your particular situation is crucial to achieving a successful result. An interview with the prospective mediator should be conducted to ascertain the mediator's background, methods and demeanor. A list of questions should be prepared in advance covering all pertinent areas of concern.

Because the mediator is a neutral party, he or she does not advocate for either side. The mediator presents the issues in a structured and informative manner, encouraging communication and cooperation, in an effort to guide the participants to a successful resolution of their controversy.

Professional mediators often have backgrounds and hold degrees in the areas of psychology and sociology. Such experience is particularly useful when dealing with the intense display of human emotions which commonly emerge in the course of a dispute. Professional mediators may also have expertise in other related fields, however, issues may arise that are sufficiently complex to warrant hiring other professionals, such as accountants or lawyers. If so, the mediator should bring that need to the parties' attention as early as possible in the process. If you do find that legal advice is indicated due to complex issues which arise during mediation, it is important to choose a lawyer who is supportive of the mediation process, so that he or she can work with—not against—the mediator.

MODEL STANDARDS OF CONDUCT FOR MEDIATORS

The Model Standards of Conduct for Mediators were prepared from 1992 through 1994 by a joint committee composed of two delegates from the American Arbitration Association, two from the American Bar Association, and two from the Society of Professionals in Dispute Resolution. The Model Standards were an initiative of, and have been approved by, the American Arbitration Association, the Litigation Section and the Dispute Resolution Section of the American Bar Association, and the Society of Professionals in Dispute Resolution.

The purpose of this initiative was to develop a set of standards to serve as a general framework for the practice of mediation. The effort is a step in the development of the field and a tool to assist practitioners. The model standards are intended to apply to all types of mediation. It is recognized, however, that in some cases the application of these standards may be affected by laws or contractual agreements.

The model standards of conduct for mediators are intended to perform three major functions:

1. To serve as a guide for the conduct of mediators;

2. To inform the mediating parties; and

3. To promote public confidence in mediation as a process for resolving disputes.

The standards draw on existing codes of conduct for mediators and take into account issues and problems that have surfaced in mediation practice. They are offered in the hope that they will serve an educational function and provide assistance to individuals, organizations, and institutions involved in mediation.

The Model Standards of Conduct for Mediators is set forth at Appendix 5.

THE MEDIATOR'S ROLE: THE 12 STAGES OF MEDIATION

Stage 1: Making Initial Contacts with the Disputing Parties

1. Make initial contact with parties.

2. Build credibility.

3. Promote rapport.

4. Educate the parties about the mediation process.

5. Increase commitment to the procedure.

Stage 2: Select a Strategy to Guide Mediation Process

1. Assist the parties in assessing the various approaches to conflict management and resolution.

2. Assist the parties in selecting an approach.

3. Coordinate the approaches of the parties.

Stage 3: Collect and Analyze Background Information

1. Collect and analyze relevant data about the people, dynamics and substance of the conflict.

2. Verify the accuracy of the data.

3. Minimize the impact of inaccurate or unavailable data.

Stage 4: Design a Detailed Plan for Mediation

1. Identify strategies and consequent noncontingent moves that will enable the parties to move toward agreement.

2. Identify contingent moves to respond to situations peculiar to the specific conflict.

Stage 5: Build Trust and Cooperation

1. Prepare disputants psychologically to participate in negotiations on substantive issues.

2. Handle strong emotions.

3. Check perceptions and minimize effects of stereotypes.

4. Build recognition of the legitimacy of the parties and issues.

5. Build trust.

6. Clarify communications.

Stage 6: Begin the Mediation Session

1. Open the negotiation between the parties.

2. Establish an open and positive tone.

3. Establish ground rules and behavior guidelines.

4. Assist the parties in venting emotions.

5. Delineate topic areas and issues for discussion.

6. Assist the parties in exploring commitments, salience and influence.

Stage 7: Define Issues and Set Agenda

1. Identify broad topic areas of concern to the parties.

2. Obtain agreement on the issues to be discussed.

3. Determine the sequence for handling the issues.

Stage 8: Uncover Hidden Interests of the Disputing Parties

1. Identify the substantive, procedural and psychological interests of the parties.

2. Educate the parties about each other's interests.

Stage 9: Generate Settlement Options

1. Develop an awareness among the parties of the need for options.

2. Lower commitment to positions or sole alternatives.

3. Generate options using either positional or interest-based bargaining.

Stage 10: Assess Settlement Options

1. Review the interests of the parties.

2. Assess how interests can be met by available options.

3. Assess the costs and benefits of selecting options.

Stage 11: Final Bargaining

1. Reach agreement through either incremental convergence of positions, final leaps to package settlements, development of a consensual formula, or establishment of a procedural means to reach a substantive agreement.

Stage 12: Achieve Formal Settlement

1. Identify procedural steps to operationalize the agreement.

2. Establish an evaluation and monitoring procedure.

3. Formalize the settlement and create an enforcement and commitment mechanism.*

---

*   Source: Moore, Christopher W., The Mediation Process: Practical Strategies for Resolving Conflict, Jossey-Bass, Inc. Publishers, 1986

CHAPTER 4:
NEGOTIATION AND SETTLEMENT

IN GENERAL

Negotiation is the least formal method of resolving a dispute without litigation. As with arbitration and mediation, the goal of negotiation is to obtain a fair and expedient resolution of a controversy. However, the opposing parties attempt to resolve their dispute without the third party intervention of an arbitrator or mediator. Negotiation, if unsuccessful, will likely be taken to another forum, such as arbitration or litigation, although negotiation may continue during the pendency of the matter, and a settlement may be reached at any point.

KEYS TO EFFECTIVE NEGOTIATION

For negotiation to succeed, the participants must be able to openly and patiently communicate with each other, even though they may disagree. Although it may be difficult to listen to a narration of facts with which one absolutely disagrees, the ability to actively listen is the mark of a good negotiator. In addition, each party will have the chance to respond and fully express their views, particularly if that courtesy has already been extended to the opponent.

The participants should be fully prepared for negotiation, and knowledgeable of the strengths and weaknesses of their position, and be able to define and advance their argument without being offensive to the other party. A cooperative attitude has been shown to foster a positive negotiating environment.

THE PROCEDURE

Unlike other dispute resolution methods, negotiation follows no established rules or guidelines. It is entirely voluntary and conducted between the parties to the negotiation, or their representatives. There are no third party intermediaries available to assist the negotiators in reaching a settlement.

Negotiation generally begins with the establishment of the identity of the parties and the subject matter of the dispute. A general exchange of information follows, during which the participants express their objectives. Points which are not in dispute may be discovered and set aside so that the participants may focus on the actual items which need to be settled.

Once the parties are satisfied that they have ascertained the pertinent information, the demand/offer/counter-offer phase begins, during which the participants attempt to justify their position, and show the other party how their method of settlement may be beneficial to both parties. Once the participants find some common ground, they may begin to make reciprocal concessions in an effort to find ways to mutually satisfy their respective objectives.

Negotiation may fail if the parties reach a stalemate in their deliberation. However, if an impasse occurs on one or more issues of the dispute, it may be helpful to change the focus of the negotiation to those issues which are closer to resolution than to forcefully attempt to break the impasse. If at least one sub-issue can be resolved, this will assist in reopening the other issues. If there are no other issues to be resolved except for those which appear to be deadlocked, it is best to end the negotiation session and schedule another session to give the participants time to contemplate their positions and alternatives.

The effective negotiator is willing to openly recognize their opponent's attempts at resolving the dispute, however insignificant those attempts may seem. In effect, this is a boost to the opponent's self-esteem and a reasonable reaction to such recognition would be for the opponent to make even greater concessions. Thus, negotiation presents a scenario of offers and counter-offers concerning resolution of a particular dispute, until the parties reach that magic middle ground on which they can mutually agree—the settlement.

SETTLEMENT

The goal of negotiation is to reach an agreement between the parties, which fairly resolves the dispute, i.e., a settlement. A controversy may be "settled" at any stage of a dispute resolution proceeding, including litigation. A settlement may be judicial or non-judicial. A non-judicial settlement is one which is reached between the parties without court intervention. A judicial settlement is one which is reached during the pendency of a lawsuit, usually with the supervision and guidance of the trial judge. In general, the policy of all courts is to encourage settlement and discourage litigation.

Once an agreement has been reached, a final written document encompassing all of the negotiated points should be drafted and signed by the parties. Depending on the nature of the dispute, a settlement agreement may also include a release of claims. By signing a release, a party gives up all right to pursue the claims stated in the release. This is both the motivation and consideration for entering into the settlement agreement.

A sample settlement agreement and release of claims is set forth at Appendix 18.

TYPES OF SETTLEMENTS

A settlement is an agreement which is tailored to the individual needs of the parties who structure the agreement. The major types of settlement agreements are detailed below.

Lump Sum Settlement

The lump sum settlement is the most common type of settlement, which generally requires the payment of a sum of money in exchange for the release of the other party's claims.

Sliding-Scale Settlement

A sliding scale settlement includes a condition in which it is agreed that an adjustment may be made to the settling defendant's obligation dependent upon any amounts which may ultimately be recovered from the nonsettling defendants.

Structured Settlement

The structured settlement allows for the payment of money, in installments, over a period of time. The structured settlement is usually used when the recovery is significant and the paying party is financially unable to make a lump sum payment, or in cases involving minors. Generally, the plaintiff receives payments from a trust or annuity which is funded by the defendant.

CHAPTER 5:
COMMERCIAL DISPUTE RESOLUTION

IN GENERAL

Many businesses have turned to alternative methods of dispute resolution to resolve their disputes, including but not limited to controversies concerning contract disputes, construction claims, consumer transactions, and securities transactions. The American Arbitration Association (AAA) has promulgated a particular set of arbitration rules for resolving commercial disputes. In addition, the AAA has also devised more specific sets of rules for resolving disputes in major industries, such as the construction, insurance and textile industries.

The Commercial Arbitration Rules of the AAA are set forth at Appendix 14.

Many of the contracts and agreements which are entered into in the various industries contain arbitration clauses. This does not mean that every disagreement which arises must be referred to arbitration. The parties are free to try and settle the matter informally. However, if they are unable to do so, the parties would submit the dispute to arbitration rather than litigation. Arbitration is an expedient and cost effective way in which to settle a controversy, and gives the parties a sense of control over the process because they can actively participate in the negotiation and settlement of the dispute.

THE ADVANTAGES

Alternative dispute resolution methods offer many advantages over litigation, which makes it particularly attractive in the business world. Arbitration is the most common method of alternative dispute resolution used to resolve business disputes. Some of its advantages are as follows:

Knowledge of the Industry

In litigation, the factfinder is either a judge or a jury, laypersons who generally have no experience in the field in which the dispute arises. The parties introduce the testimony of expert witnesses, who attempt to provide

---

the layperson with an understanding of the business, and how it relates to the underlying dispute.

In contrast, arbitration offers the advantage of permitting the parties to hire an arbitrator who is also an expert in the particular field, such as an architect or an engineer, depending on the subject matter of the dispute. When the parties present their case, they are able to do so in the language of the trade rather than resorting to technical and procedural legal jargon.

Time Factor

Litigation is time consuming, and can go on for many years while the parties exhaust all of their appellate remedies. Arbitration provides an expeditious resolution of the dispute, particularly since the awards are binding and final. The parties generally have no right to appeal the arbitrator's decision.

Cost Factor

The expense of litigation is very high and may include legal fees and disbursements, court filing fees and costs, expert witness fees, investigation costs, etc. A small business could go bankrupt as a result of protracted litigation. On the other hand, the cost of arbitration is generally predictable and comparatively small. The AAA charges a filing fee to defray administrative expenses. The filing fee is based on the amount of the claim. The larger the amount in dispute, the higher the filing fee will be. The parties are also responsible for paying the arbitrator's fee, and other miscellaneous expenses. In addition, the parties may contractually agree in advance on how the costs of arbitration are to be split.

Privacy

A lawsuit is generally a matter of public record, whereas arbitration is a private and confidential proceeding. This serves to avoid a scenario where the parties may be unwilling to discuss certain matters for fear of giving away a trade secret to a competitor, and avoids the bad publicity that may accompany a major lawsuit.

International Arbitration

Contracts involving international trade often contain arbitration clauses so as to eliminate the uncertainty which choice of law and jurisdiction produce. Arbitration provides the parties with a clearly defined method of resolving potential disputes because the location and applicable law can be predetermined in the contract.

A directory of the major international arbitration agencies is set forth at Appendix 2.

THE CORPORATE POLICY STATEMENT

It has been shown how the use of alternative dispute resolution methods is advantageous in numerous ways, particularly in the context of business disputes. Therefore, many businesses have adopted a corporate policy aimed at using alternative dispute methods, such as arbitration, mediation and negotiation, to resolve disputes and avoid litigation, if at all possible. For example, the mini-trial, which is discussed more fully in Chapter 1, has recently proven to be a very successful method of corporate dispute resolution in many complex commercial disputes.

A sample corporate policy statement is set forth at Appendix 19.

SECURITIES ARBITRATION

Arbitration and mediation have been useful in resolving disputes which arise in the area of securities arbitration, i.e., disagreements involving securities transactions and commodities futures. In October 1991, a Securities Task Force comprised of representatives of various brokerage firms, attorneys, and persons knowledgeable about securities matters and arbitration, was created in order to improve the existing procedures and rules relating to securities arbitration.

As a result of their efforts, the AAA's Securities Arbitration Rules were amended in May 1993, providing a more effective administration of securities arbitration matters. Included in the new rules, is an expedited system of arbitration for claims involving less than $25,000, exclusive of interest and arbitration costs.

The new rules also set forth the qualifications of industry-affiliated arbitrators, who must have direct involvement in or relationship with the securities brokerage industry for (a) a minimum of three years if now employed in the industry; or (b) a minimum of five years if no longer employed in the industry. A person who has not been employed in the industry for more than ten years is not considered industry-affiliated.

Involvement in or relationship with the securities brokerage industry is defined as (a) employment at a brokerage firm in a professional capacity, whether employed in sales, management, support or trading, or (b) employment as counsel, accountant or other professional who devotes a majority of his or her efforts to brokerage or brokerage-related matters.

CONSTRUCTION INDUSTRY ARBITRATION

Alternative dispute resolution has been broadly and successfully used by the construction industry for much of the twentieth century. The AAA administers construction claim cases arising under the arbitration provisions contained in the standard form documents of the American Institute of Architects. According to the American Arbitration Association, many thousands of construction claims involving billions of dollars were resolved privately and expeditiously through mediation and arbitration.

In addition to arbitration and mediation, new approaches to resolving disputes arising in the construction industry are being explored, including (a) the Dispute Review Board; and (b) Partnering.

The Dispute Review Board

The creation of a Dispute Review Board to oversee ongoing construction is a consensual process, which offers an early resolution of disputes which may arise during the course of the project. A Dispute Review Board consists of three neutral and objective members, who are selected and approved by both the contractor and the owner. The Board members are experienced in the construction industry. The Board is kept informed as construction progresses. If a problem arises during construction, the Board is notified. The Board makes appropriate recommendations to settle such disputes as they arise. It is expected that the parties will accept the Board's non-binding recommendation. The advantage of this method of dispute resolution is that it provides early intervention, which is crucial in the context of a construction dispute, as delays of long duration can effectively destroy a construction project.

Partnering

Partnering, as defined by the Construction Industry Institute, is a long-term commitment between two or more organizations for the purpose of achieving their specific business objectives by maximizing the effectiveness of each participant's resources. In short, partnering involves close communication among all of the parties to a particular construction project, in a common effort to complete the project in a cost-efficient and expeditious manner, i.e., "teamwork."

Before the construction project begins, all of the parties are encouraged to participate in a partnering workshop, in an effort to get to know each other on a personal level. During the workshop, the services of a neutral third party, known as a facilitator, are often utilized. The facilitator is one who is experienced in developing team-building skills. In addition, the facilitator is knowledgeable in the construction industry. The facilitator helps the parties identify their goals and devise a "partnering charter" which sets forth the agreed upon methods of resolving disputes which may arise as construction progresses.

The American Arbitration Association offers support and services to parties who wish to use the partnering method of dispute resolution. The AAA provides education and training programs on partnering workshops, and will appoint a qualified facilitator to conduct the workshop.

THE NEW YORK LEMON LAW ARBITRATION PROGRAM

An example of an arbitration program designed to address consumer transactions is the New York State Lemon Law Arbitration Program ("The Lemon Law"). The Lemon Law has provided a legal remedy for the purchasers and lessees of new cars, and covered used cars, that turn out to be "lemons." The consumer has the right to sue (i) the auto manufacturer of a new car; or (ii) the dealer of a used car.

The law also provides an alternative which allows the consumer to participate in the arbitration procedure to resolve the dispute. In order to implement this law without unnecessarily overwhelming the court with additional litigation, New York State has established a Lemon Law Arbitration Program which is administered by the American Arbitration Association (AAA) under regulations issued by the Attorney General.

Various auto manufacturers and dealers have established their own arbitration programs. The law permits them to require consumers to participate in an in-house arbitration proceeding before the consumer is permitted to sue in court, provided the in-house proceeding complies with the state's lemon law and the federal regulations. However, the decisions reached in those proceedings are not binding on the consumer. This means that if the consumer is not happy with the outcome of that proceeding, he or she may still elect to submit the dispute to the AAA under the New York Lemon Law Arbitration Program. The decisions rendered in the New York Lemon Law Arbitration Program are binding on both parties, subject only to limited judicial review under New York law.

The New Car Lemon Law

Pursuant to General Business Law, Section 198-a, the New Car Lemon Law provides a legal remedy for consumers who buy or lease a new car and certain used cars, from automobile dealers, which turn out to be defective. This right cannot be waived in the contract, and any contract clause which attempts to waive this right is void.

A car is covered under this provision if:

1. The car was covered by the manufacturer's new car warranty at the time of original delivery; and

2. The car was purchased, leased or transferred within the earlier of the first 18,000 miles or two years from the date of original delivery; and

3. The car either (a) was purchased, leased or transferred in New York, or (b) is presently registered in New York; and

4. The car is primarily used for personal purposes.

If the car does not conform to the terms of the written warranty, and the consumer is still experiencing problems with the vehicle after a reasonable number of repair attempts by the manufacturer or its authorized dealer during the earlier of the first 18,000 miles or two years, the consumer is entitled to a full refund or a comparable replacement car.

The Used Car Lemon Law

Pursuant to General Business Law, Section 198-b, the Used Car Lemon Law provides a legal remedy for consumers who buy or lease certain covered used cars from automobile dealers, which turn out to be defective. This right also cannot be waived in the contract, and any contract clause which attempts to waive this right is void. Furthermore, a dealer is prohibited from selling a covered used car in an "as is" condition.

A used car is covered under this provision if:

1. It was purchased, leased or transferred after the earlier of (a) 18,000 miles of operation or (b) two years from the date of original delivery; and

2. It was purchased or leased from a New York dealer; and

3. It had a purchase price or lease value of at least $1,500; and

4. It had been driven less than 100,000 miles at the time of purchase or lease; and

5. It is primarily used for personal purposes.

A used car purchased or leased with 18,000 miles or less, and within two years from the date of original delivery, is covered by the New Car Lemon Law, as set forth above. The law also covers persons to whom the used car was transferred by the purchaser during the used car lemon law warranty period. The law does not cover the private sales of automobiles.

The Used Car Lemon Law requires the dealer to give the consumer a written warranty which states that the dealer must repair, free of charge, any defects in certain specified covered parts. If the consumer is still experiencing problems with the vehicle after a reasonable number of repair attempts, the consumer is entitled to a full refund.

The warranty period on a covered used car is based on the mileage at the time of purchase or lease, as follows:

1. Cars with 18,001 to 36,000 miles at the time of purchase or lease are covered until the earlier of 90 days or 4,000 miles has elapsed;

2. Cars with 36,001 to 79,999 miles at the time of purchase or lease are covered until the earlier of 60 days or 3,000 miles has elapsed;

2. Cars with 80,000 to 100,000 miles at the time of purchase or lease are covered until the earlier of 30 days or 1,000 miles has elapsed.

The warranty period is extended for each day that the car is in the shop being repaired.

The Proceeding

The New York State New and Used Lemon Law Arbitration Program is administered by the American Arbitration Association (the "AAA Program") under regulations issued by the Attorney General. Decisions rendered after the proceeding are binding on the parties. If the consumer chooses to participate in the in-house arbitration program established by the automobile dealer, if any, the decision in that proceeding is not binding and the consumer still has the right to apply for arbitration under the AAA Program.

In order to initiate arbitration under the AAA Program, the consumer must file a request for arbitration with the Attorney General's office. Upon review of the request, the Attorney General's office will determine whether the consumer is eligible for arbitration under the law. If so, the request is forwarded to the AAA, who contacts the consumer. The consumer is required to forward a filing fee to the AAA, who then appoints an arbitrator and schedules a hearing. The hearing is generally held within 35 days from receipt of the filing fee.

The consumer has a right to an oral hearing in which to present his or her case before an arbitrator who has been specially trained in this area of law. The consumer may be represented by an attorney, but it is not necessary. Alternatively, the consumer may request that the hearing be conducted by review of the documentation only. However, if the manufacturer and/or dealer objects to a "documents only" hearing, then an oral hearing will be held.

A decision is rendered approximately 10 days following the hearing. If the consumer is victorious, the manufacturer and/or dealer must comply with the arbitrator's decision within 30 days or face penalties. The consumer is also entitled to the refund of his or her filing fee from the manufacturer and/or dealer.

The arbitrator's decision is final and binding, however, in certain limited circumstances, either party may initiate a lawsuit to challenge the arbitrator's award. This must be done within 90 days of receipt of the award. Nevertheless, if the arbitrator's decision was reasonable and supported by evidence, a court will not likely overturn the arbitrator's award.

CHAPTER 6:
EMPLOYMENT DISPUTE RESOLUTION

IN GENERAL

According to the American Arbitration Association (AAA), nearly 400 companies and 4 million employees worldwide turn to the American Arbitration Association to resolve workplace conflicts. The AAA maintains a national panel of experts who have significant employment law experience to hear these disputes. The experts encompass many ethnicities and both genders. To avoid the time and expense of litigation, an increasing number of employers are turning to these alternative dispute resolution procedures to resolve non-union workplace disputes.

THE USE OF ADR IN THE WORKPLACE

Federal and state laws have been enacted to protect the employee in the workplace. Thus, employers are facing liability under a number of statutory schemes which simply did not exist before. Liability may arise in the context of wrongful termination, sexual harassment, or discrimination based on race, color, religion, sex, national origin, age and/or disability. However, because courts and administrative agencies are becoming overburdened with cases, the employee is facing an extraordinarily long wait before their case can be heard.

Therefore, alternative dispute resolution has emerged as a prompt and effective way to resolve workplace disputes. Alternative dispute resolution procedures are more readily found in employment contracts, and in employee handbooks and materials.

EMPLOYMENT DISCRIMINATION ISSUES

In the Americans with Disabilities Act and in Section 118 of the Civil Rights Act of 1991, Congress has stated that the ADR plays an important role in the area of employment discrimination. In addition, the Supreme Court upheld an arbitration agreement which the employee was required to sign as a condition of employment, finding that the Age Discrimination in Employment Act did not preclude arbitration of age discrimination claims (Gilmer v. Interstate/Johnson Lane, 500 U.S. 20, 111 S.Ct. 1647 (1991). In addition, lower federal courts have generally enforced employer-imposed alternative dispute resolution programs provided the programs are fair and afford the employee due process.

The Due Process Protocol for Mediation and Arbitration of Statutory Disputes Arising Out of the Employment Relationship was developed in 1995 by a special task force composed of individuals representing management, labor, employment, civil rights organizations, private administrative agencies, government, and the American Arbitration Association.

The Due Process Protocol, which was endorsed by the Association in 1995, seeks to ensure fairness and equity in resolving workplace disputes. The Due Process Protocol encourages mediation and arbitration of statutory disputes, provided there are due process safeguards. It has been endorsed by organizations representing a broad range of constituencies, including the American Arbitration Association, the American Bar Association Labor and Employment Section, the American Civil Liberties Union, the Federal Mediation and Conciliation Service, the National Academy of Arbitrators, and the Society of Professionals in Dispute Resolution.

The National Employment Lawyers Association has also endorsed the substantive provisions of the Due Process Protocol, which has also been incorporated into the ADR procedures of the Massachusetts Commission Against Discrimination (MCAD) and into the Report of the United States Secretary of Labor's Task Force on Excellence in State and Local Government.

AAA EMPLOYMENT DISPUTE RESOLUTION RULES

The AAA's policy on alternative dispute resolution in the area of employment is guided by the state of existing law, as well as its obligation to act in an impartial manner. In following the law, and in the interest of providing an appropriate forum for the resolution of employment disputes, the AAA administers dispute resolution programs which meet the due process standards as outlined in its National Rules for the Resolution of Employment Disputes and the Due Process Protocol.

If the AAA determines that a dispute resolution program on its face substantially and materially deviates from the minimum due process standards of the National Rules for the Resolution of Employment Disputes and the Due Process Protocol, the AAA will decline to administer cases under that program.

ALTERNATIVE DISPUTE RESOLUTION OPTIONS FOR EMPLOYERS

The AAA suggests the following alternative dispute resolution options for employers:

Open Door Policy

Employees are encouraged to meet with their immediate manager or supervisor to discuss problems arising out of the workplace environment. In some systems, the employee is free to approach anyone in the chain of command.

Ombuds

A neutral third party is designated to confidentially investigate and propose settlement of employment complaints brought by employees.

Peer Review

A panel of employees works together to resolve employment complaints. Peer review panel members are trained in the handling of sensitive issues.

Internal Mediation

A process for resolving disputes in which a neutral third person from within the company, trained in mediation techniques, helps the disputing parties negotiate a mutually acceptable settlement. Mediation is a nonbinding process.

Factfinding

The investigation of a complaint by an impartial third person who examines the complaint and the facts and issues a non-binding report. As set forth below, fact-finding is particularly helpful for allegations of sexual harassment, where a fact-finding team, composed of one male and one female neutral, investigates the allegations and presents its findings to the employer and the employee.

External Mediation

The AAA recommends an external mediation component to resolve disputes not settled by the internal dispute resolution process. The National Rules for the Resolution of Employment Disputes have a mediation component to foster the use of this method of dispute resolution, and the AAA encourages parties to use mediation even where a case is commenced under an arbitration clause.

Mediation is a process in which the parties discuss their dispute with an impartial person who assists them in reaching a settlement. The mediator may suggest ways of resolving the dispute but may not impose a settlement on the parties. The AAA has developed a roster of experienced mediators knowledgeable in the employment field. It assists the parties in selecting the right mediator for their dispute, and in scheduling a meeting.

Arbitration

Disputes not resolved by the outside mediation step can be arbitrated. Arbitration is generally defined as the submission of a dispute to one or more impartial persons for final and binding determination. It can be the final step in a workplace program that includes other dispute resolution methods. There are many possibilities for designing this final step. Programs which use arbitration as a final step may employ the following options:

Pre-Dispute/Final and Binding Arbitration

The parties agree in advance to use arbitration to resolve disputes and they are bound by the outcome. Where clear notice has been given to employees when plans containing a mandatory arbitration component are implemented, and where the plan is fair, courts have generally enforced them.

Pre-Dispute/Nonbinding Arbitration

The parties agree in advance to use arbitration to resolve disputes, but they are not bound by the outcome.

Post-Dispute/Final and Binding Arbitration

The parties have the option of deciding to arbitrate unresolved disputes after a dispute arises, and they are bound by the outcome.

Post-Dispute/Nonbinding Arbitration.

The parties have the option of deciding to arbitrate unresolved disputes after a dispute arises, but they are not bound by the outcome.

SEXUAL HARASSMENT CLAIMS

Sexual harassment claims have traditionally been handled through an adversarial process. Because they often deal with situations involving ongoing relationships between employees and employers or between coworkers, an inquisitorial approach is frequently ineffective. It is difficult to ascertain who is telling the truth or what the truth is. A direct challenge to the veracity of persons in the same workplace interferes with their future ability to work together.

To create more appropriate methods of resolving these disputes, the AAA convened a working group representing the full spectrum of points of view in this field—large and small employers, unions, the plaintiff's employment bar, the alternative dispute resolution discipline, and an organizational dynamics perspective. This group worked for a year to understand and meld the different perspectives.

This process has been designed to address the needs of the accuser, the accused, and the employer. It is a model that can be adopted by employers in whole or with modifications. The AAA believes that this model process will provide for more efficient and sensitive resolution of sexual harassment claims.

The Model Sexual Harassment Claim Resolution Process

Complaint and Answer

The Model Sexual Harassment Claim Resolution Process is initiated when a designated manager receives a written or oral complaint of sexual harassment from, or on behalf of, an Accuser.

Confidentiality

At this stage, confidentiality is to be maintained to the greatest extent possible, both about the fact that the complaint has been made and its investigation. Information will be conveyed on a "need to know" basis. Violation of the confidentiality provision may compromise the resolution process.

Documentation

Written documentation of the complaint of sexual harassment should be made, including as many details as possible. The Accuser must sign the form and is given a copy.

Accuser Participation Agreement

The Accuser must agree, in writing, to participate in the resolution process and abide by its terms, including a confidentiality provision affirming that the neutral factfinders may not be called as witnesses in any later proceeding.

Notification to the Accused

The Accused will be notified and provided a copy of the Complaint. The Accused will be encouraged to provide a written Answer to the Complaint, responding to all allegations.

Accused Participation Agreement

The Accused must agree, in writing, to participate in the resolution process, and abide by its terms, including a confidentiality provision affirming that the neutral factfinders may not be called as witnesses in any later proceeding.

Immediate Intervention

If it appears that intervention is necessary to prevent any continued harassment, whatever action is necessary will be taken.

Request for Fact Finders

The factfinding process will be initiated by contacting the AAA and making a request for appointment of a factfinding team. The Request shall be in writing and shall contain the name, address and telephone number of Employer, the Accuser, the union, if any, and the Accused, if known. The following should be attached to the Request—a copy of the Complaint and the Answer; the agreements signed by the Accuser and the Accused; and, if any of the following exists, a copy of the contract, collective-bargaining agreement, hand book, dispute resolution policies and procedures, or sexual harassment policies and procedures pursuant to which the request is being made by the Employer. By submitting this request, the Employer agrees to participate in the process; agrees to keep the matter as confidential as possible; and also agrees that the neutral factfinders who will conduct the investigation may not be called as witnesses in any later proceeding.

Fact Finding

Appointment of the Factfinding Team

A neutral factfinding team will be appointed to investigate the Complaint and issue a written report of its findings. The factfinding team will be composed of one female and one male.

Disclosure

Any person appointed as a factfinder shall disclose any circumstance likely to affect impartiality, including any bias or any financial or personal interest in the result of the factfinding or any past or present relationship with the parties or their representatives. Upon receipt of this information from the factfinders or another source, it shall be communicated to the Employer, the Accuser, and the Accused and, if it deems it appropriate to do so, to the factfinders and others. Either the Employer, the Accuser, or the Accused may object to the factfinding team for cause within one business day after receiving notice of its appointment. Upon objection of the Employer, the Accuser, or the Accused to the service of a factfinder, a determination will be made as to whether the factfinder should be disqualified and the Employer, the Accuser, and the Accused shall be informed of the decision, which shall be conclusive.

Investigation

The factfinding team will conduct joint interviews of persons who have information concerning the alleged harassment. It will interview both the Accuser and the Accused. In an extensive hostile-environment Complaint, all persons who fall with in the category of the Accused must be interviewed. Witnesses who are identified by the Accuser and the Accused will also be interviewed. During these factfinding interviews, no lawyer may be present representing any party. The Employer, the Accuser, and the Accused are expected to cooperate by making themselves and persons over whom they have influence and control available to answer all questions directed to them fully and factually. The factfinding team will have access to all relevant information and documents. The investigation and the delivery of the factfinding report will be completed within two weeks after the appointment of the team.

The Factfinding Report

The factfinding report will be concise and written in plain English. It will summarize the facts found by the factfinding team and identify the factual issues on which the team cannot agree. It will reach no conclusion as to whether there has or has not been sexual harassment. It will not recommend a remedy. The report will include credibility determinations only where both of the factfinders are in agreement. In the report, close questions of credibility may be identified and explanations included as to the circumstances that make them close questions.

Report Distribution

The factfinding team will provide the report to the AAA, which will provide it to Employer, the Accuser, and the Accused. The Accuser and the Accused will receive the report whether or not they are currently employed by the Employer when it is issued and distributed. Where the Complaint involves extensive hostile-environment allegations, the Employer may limit distribution of the report to only the Accused who are the primary subjects of the investigation and the findings. All employees who are provided a copy of the report should be advised of their obligation of confidentiality. Before they receive the report, they will be required to sign a confidentiality provision similar to the one signed by the Accuser at the initiation of the process.

Mediation

If a mutually satisfactory resolution is not reached on or before thirty days after receipt of the factfinding report, the process shall proceed to mediation at the request of the Employer, the Accuser, or the Accused. If the process has proceeded without the Accuser's agreement to mediation, the Accuser should again be requested to agree to participate in the mediation phase of the process. If the process has proceeded without the Accused's agreement to mediation, the Accused should again be requested to agree to participate in the mediation phase of the process.

Appointment of a Mediator

The AAA will appoint a mediator. The mediator may be of either gender but will not be one of the factfinders unless agreed by all of the parties.

Disclosure

Any person appointed as a mediator shall disclose to the AAA any circumstance likely to affect impartiality, including any bias or any financial or personal interest in the result of the mediation or any past or present relationship with the parties or their representatives. Upon receipt of this information from the mediator or another source, the AAA shall communicate the information to the Employer, the Accuser, and the Accused and, if it deems it appropriate to do so, to the mediator and others. The Accuser, the Accused, or the Employer may object to the mediator for good cause within one business day after the appointment. Upon objection of the Employer, the Accuser, or the Accused to the service of a mediator, the AAA shall either replace the mediator or immediately communicate the information to the parties for their comments. In the event that the parties disagree as to whether the mediator shall serve, the AAA will appoint another mediator. The AAA is authorized to appoint another mediator if the appointed mediator is unable to serve promptly.

Mediation Procedure

Except as superseded by this process, the AAA's Employment Mediation Rules will be followed in conducting the mediation. Mediation will begin on or before thirty days after appointment of the mediator. The AAA may extend this time limit but only for good cause. The AAA will provide the mediator with a copy of the factfinding report. All of the parties are expected to engage in the mediation in good faith.

Arbitration

If mediation is unsuccessful in resolving the dispute, the process may proceed to arbitration.

Selection of an Arbitrator

There will be one neutral arbitrator of either gender. The AAA will submit simultaneously to each party an identical list of five proposed arbitrators drawn from the National Panel of Sexual Harassment Claim Arbitrators, from which one arbitrator shall be appointed. Each party may strike two names from the list on a peremptory basis. The list is returnable to the AAA within seven days after the AAA mails the list to the parties. If for any reason the appointment of an arbitrator cannot be made from the list, the AAA may make the appointment from among other members of the panel without submitting additional lists. The AAA will notify the parties by telephone of the appointment of the arbitrator.

Disclosure

Any person appointed as a neutral arbitrator shall disclose to the AAA any circumstance likely to affect impartiality, including any bias or any financial or personal interest in the result of the arbitration or any past or present relationship with the parties or their representatives. Upon receipt of this information from the arbitrator or another source, the AAA shall communicate the information to the Employer, the Accuser, and the Accused and, if it deems it appropriate to do so, to the arbitrator and others. Within seven days, the parties shall notify the AAA, by telephone, of any objection to the arbitrator appointed. Any objection by a party to the arbitrator shall be confirmed in writing to the AAA with a copy to the other parties. Upon objection of the Employer, the Accuser, or the Accused to the service of a neutral arbitrator, the AAA shall determine whether the arbitrator should be disqualified and shall inform the parties of its decision, which shall be conclusive.

Arbitration Procedures

Except as superseded by this process, the expedited procedures of the AAA Employment Dispute Resolution Rules will be followed in conducting the arbitration. The arbitration shall begin on or before thirty days after the appointment of the arbitrator.

Employee/Witness Wages

The Employer shall pay the wages of current employees who are subpoenaed for the arbitration for the time that they spend appearing and testifying in the arbitration, to the extent that they would otherwise have been working.

Remedies

The arbitrator shall have broad powers to award appropriate remedies consistent with Title VII of the Civil Rights Act of 1964, as amended.

The Arbitrator's Decision and Award

The results of the arbitration shall be reported to all parties in writing on or before thirty days after the closing of the evidence. The award shall contain a brief summary of the facts upon which the arbitrator based the award. All parties shall be bound by the arbitrator's decision, which decision shall be enforceable pursuant to applicable law.

CHAPTER 7:
AUTOMOBILE INSURANCE CLAIM DISPUTE RESOLUTION

DISPUTE RESOLUTION OF AUTOMOBILE INSURANCE CLAIMS

Parties can generally agree to submit an automobile insurance claim dispute to arbitration or mediation with the American Arbitration Association under their rules and procedures. By mutual agreement, in writing, the parties may modify any provision. Cases may be initiated by a joint submission in writing, containing a brief description of the dispute and the names and addresses of the parties, together with the applicable filing fee.

A sample AAA Arbitration Request Form under the New York State Motor Vehicle No-Fault Insurance Law is set forth at Appendix 20.

Automobile insurance policies written in every state protect an insured against personal injury caused by uninsured and hit-and-run motorists. The standard uninsured motorist endorsement is one in which the insurer promises to pay all sums which the insured shall be legally entitled to recover as damages from the owner or operator of an uninsured automobile, which result from the bodily injury sustained by the insured. The injuries must have been caused by the accident and arise out of the ownership, maintenance or use of the uninsured automobile. Determination as to whether the insured is legally entitled to recover such damages and, if so, the amount thereof, shall be made by agreement between the insured and the company or, if they fail to agree, by arbitration.

This endorsement typically contains a provision for arbitration, which generally reads as follows:

> If any person making claim hereunder and the company do not agree that such person is legally entitled to recover damages from the owner or operator of an uninsured automobile because of the amount of payment which may be owing under this endorsement, then, upon written demand of either, the matter or matters upon which such person and the company do not agree shall be settled by arbitration in accordance

with the rules of the American Arbitration Association, and judgment upon the award rendered by the arbitrators may be entered in any court having jurisdiction thereof. Such person and the company each agree to consider itself bound and to be bound by any award made by the arbitrators pursuant to this endorsement.

In 1956, at the request of the insurance industry, the American Arbitration Association established the following procedures for arbitrating automobile insurance claims:

Mediation

The AAA encourages parties to submit their accident claim disputes to mediation, which has proven to be a prompt, fair, and economical method of resolving insurance claims. The mediation provisions of the AAA's Alternative Dispute Resolution Procedures for Insurance Claims will be utilized where the parties agree to mediate their dispute.

In mediation, the mediator assists the parties in reaching their own settlement, but does not have the authority to make a binding decision or award. Mediators appointed under this program are experienced attorneys. They have specific training or experience in mediation and are prepared to offer prompt service. The AAA makes every effort to appoint mediators who are acceptable to both parties. Upon the objection of either party, the AAA will replace a mediator.

Because mediation is voluntary, all parties to the dispute must consent to participate. If there is no agreement to mediate or if mediation proves unsuccessful, the parties can continue with arbitration, as set forth below.

Arbitration

The AAA maintains an Accident Claims Panel of arbitrators made up of attorneys with negligence experience. Each of the AAA's regional offices maintains an Advisory Committee, made up of equal numbers of at least three members of the defense bar and/or the insurance industry and three members of the plaintiff's bar, which will approve the qualifications of the members of that panel. Each committee shall meet at least once a year.

When the conditions precedent contained in the insurance policy or state insurance-department regulations have been complied with, arbitration shall be initiated by filing a written Demand for Arbitration. The demand shall be served by certified mail-return receipt requested. When filed by an insured, it shall be directed to the claims office of the insurer under whose policy arbitration is sought, at the office where the claim has been discussed, or at the office of the insurer closest to the residence of the insured.

The demand shall set forth the following information:

(1) the name, address, and telephone number of the insured person(s) and the filing attorney;

(2) the name, address and policy number of the policyholder;

(3) the identity and location of the claims office of the insurer, if known; the claim's file number, if known; and the name of the individual with whom the claim was discussed;

(4) the date and location of the accident;

(5) the nature of dispute and injuries alleged;

(6) the amount of uninsured-motorist policy limits and the amount claimed thereunder; and,

(7) the address of the AAA regional office at which copies of the demand are being filed.

Three copies of the demand must be filed with an AAA regional office at the same time, with a copy of the parts of the policy or regulations relating to the dispute, including the arbitration provisions, together with the administrative filing fee.

The AAA will acknowledge receipt of the demand to all parties. If, within thirty calendar days after acknowledgment of the demand by the AAA, the insured moves in court to contest coverage, applicable policy limits, or stacking of policy coverage, administration will be suspended until such issues are decided.

All issues covering compliance with conditions precedent may be decided by an arbitrator. Issues as to applicable policy limits, or stacking of policy coverage may be referred to voluntary coverage arbitration with the agreement of all parties before an arbitrator appointed by the AAA from a panel designated to hear such issues. These issues will be submitted to the arbitrator on documents only, unless the parties agree otherwise or the arbitrator determines that an oral hearing is necessary.

In the absence of an agreement to submit such issues to arbitration, accident claims arbitrators may only decide contested issues of coverage, applicable policy limits, or stacking of policy coverage where ordered to do so by a court or where so authorized by law.

Unless there is (1) an agreement to submit such issues to voluntary coverage arbitration, (2) a motion to contest coverage, applicable policy limits, or the stacking of policy coverage made within thirty calendar days after acknowledgment of the demand by the AAA, or (3) a court order staying arbitration, the AAA will proceed with the administration of the case.

Either the county of residence of the insured or the county where the accident occurred may be designated by the insured as the locale in which the hearing is to be held. Only if all parties agree shall the hearing be held in some other locale.

Unless applicable law or the agreement of the parties provides otherwise, the dispute is determined by one arbitrator. The AAA submits a list of nine members of the Accident Claims Panel from which each party has the right to strike up to two names on a peremptory basis, within twenty days of the AAA's submission of the list. The AAA will appoint the arbitrator from among the remaining names.

Where the amount claimed and available coverage limits exceed minimum statutory financial responsibility limits, upon the request of a party made within thirty calendar days after acknowledgment of the demand by the AAA, the dispute shall be determined by three arbitrators. The AAA will then submit a list of thirteen names from the Accident Claims Panel, allowing each party to strike up to three names on a peremptory basis, within twenty days of the AAA's submission of the list. The AAA will appoint three arbitrators from among the remaining names.

If the parties fail to agree on any of the persons named on the list of arbitrators, if acceptable arbitrators are unable to act, or if for any other reason the appointment cannot be made from the submitted lists, the AAA shall have the power to make the appointment from among other members of the panel without submitting additional lists.

The arbitrator fixes the time and place for each hearing. The AAA mails a notice to each party at least twenty calendar days in advance. Any party may be represented by counsel or other authorized representative.

CHAPTER 8:
HEALTH CARE DISPUTE RESOLUTION

IN GENERAL

It has become increasingly evident that some type of alternative dispute resolution system is needed to provide the public with a more expedient manner in which to have their health care disputes resolved without having to resort to litigation. As courts and administrative agencies become less accessible to civil litigants, patients, health care providers, and managed care and health plan programs have begun to explore alternative dispute resolution as a way to promptly and effectively resolve disputes. A wide range of dispute prevention and resolution procedures allow the participants to develop a fair, cost-effective, and private forum to resolve disputes.

In response to this concern, in August 1997, leaders of the American Arbitration Association (AAA), American Bar Association (ABA), and American Medical Association (AMA) met in Chicago and determined to form a commission to study and make recommendations on the appropriate use of alternative dispute resolution in the private health plan/managed care environment. The Commission's goal is to engage health care providers in this effort. The Commission will not study the applicability of ADR to medical malpractice, Medicare, or general access to health care outside of the private health plan/managed-care relationship.

OBJECTIVES

The objectives of the Commission are:

1. Studying and making recommendations on the application of alternative dispute resolution for coverage and access issues in the managed care arena, including:

(a) access to specific health care providers;

(b) access to needed treatment;

(c) access to specific health care facilities;

(d) medical necessity of treatment;

(e) experimental treatment;

(f) reasonableness of cost;

(g) continuity of care;

(h) disclosure of information to consumers;

(i) development of drug formularies;

(j) out-of-area coverage;

(k) provider communication with patients; and

(l) utilization management.

2. The development of appropriate due process standards; and

3. The development of model ADR procedures that can be utilized in the managed care relationship.

ALTERNATIVE DISPUTE RESOLUTION METHODS

The following ADR procedures have been suggested as appropriate alternative methods of resolving disputes in the health care environment:

1. Ombuds: A neutral third party is designated to receive information regarding disputes from users of managed care and health plans and to confidentially investigate and propose settlement of complaints brought by patients.

2. Fact-finding: The investigation of a complaint by an impartial third person who examines the complaint, considers the facts ascertained, and issues a non-binding report.

3. Mediation: The process in which the parties discuss their disputes with an impartial person who assists them in reaching a settlement. The mediator may suggest ways of resolving the dispute but may not impose a settlement on the parties. Mediation offers the advantage of informality, with reduced time and expense needed to resolve disputes.

4. Arbitration: The submission of disputes to one or more impartial persons pursuant to established procedures, for final and binding determination.

In developing appropriate ADR methods, the Commission has consulted with health care providers, patient advocacy groups, public health officials and groups, elder care groups, and law and medical school faculty.

CHAPTER 9:
LABOR RELATIONS DISPUTE RESOLUTION

LABOR ARBITRATION

Federal arbitration statutes relating to labor-management relations began being enacted by Congress in the early twentieth century. In 1925, the United States Arbitration Act was enacted, which declared that arbitration clauses contained in contracts involving interstate commerce were enforceable. In 1926, The Railway Labor Act stated that arbitration would be the means by which employment disputes between railroads and their workers were to be resolved. In 1943, the War Labor Disputes Act held that arbitration would be the means by which labor disputes were resolved in industries related to national defense.

The National Labor Relations Board (NLRB) is an independent agency created by the National Labor Relations Act of 1935, also known as the Wagner Act, which was subsequently amended in 1947 by the Taft-Hartley Labor-Management Relations Act, and again in 1959 by the Landrum-Griffin Act. The principal functions of the NLRB are to prevent and remedy unfair labor practices by employers and labor unions, and to conduct secret ballot elections among employees belonging to particular collective bargaining units, to determine whether the employees desire union representation or, if already represented, if the employees want to change unions.

The NLRB is statutorily required to employ the arbitration process to resolve all disputes between union and management concerning unfair labor practices. The contracts between union and management are reached through what is known as the collective bargaining process. This refers to the right of an uncoerced majority of the employees within a particular bargaining unit to be represented by a designated bargaining agent in contract negotiations. An arbitrator may be utilized to declare the respective rights of the party if they are unable to agree to the terms of a prospective contract, or if a dispute arises under an existing contract.

Many states also require that labor-management disputes, particularly those involving civil service employees, be submitted to arbitration, and most collective bargaining agreements contain arbitration clauses. Arbitration is also a popular means of resolving private labor-related disputes, such as those arising in the field of professional sports between the team owners and the players.

LABOR MEDIATION

Mediation is also used in settling labor disputes where the parties are generally conciliatory and willing to mediate the dispute. In such a case, the more formal process of arbitration is not considered necessary unless an impasse occurs in the bargaining process.

In 1934, the National Mediation Board was established by an act of Congress which amended the Railway Labor Act (48 Stat. 1185, 45 U.S.C.A. §§ 151-158,160-162). The Board's major responsibilities include the mediation of disputes over wages, hours and working conditions, which arise between rail and air carriers and the organizations representing their employees. The Board also investigates union representation disputes, and certification of employee organizations as representatives of crafts or classes of carrier employees.

In 1947, the Federal Mediation and Conciliation Service (FMCS) was established as an independent department of the federal government organized under 29 U.S.C.A. § 172 et seq., for the purpose of settling labor disputes through conciliation and mediation. The FMCS helps prevent disruptions in the flow of interstate commerce caused by labor disputes. It provides mediators to assist the parties in settling disputes. The FMCS has the authority to intervene in a labor dispute on its own motion, and may also be asked to participate in the dispute by either party. The FMCS is beneficial to the public interest because it promotes stability between management and labor by encouraging the settlement of disputes through alternative dispute resolution methods.

State legislatures have also enacted legislation which includes mediation as a means of settling labor-management disputes.

CHAPTER 10:
DIVORCE AND FAMILY RELATIONS
DISPUTE RESOLUTION

IN GENERAL

Divorce is an emotionally devastating experience for the couple who has made the decision to end their marriage. This is true even in situations where the decision to part is mutually agreed upon. There are almost always areas of contention which need to be resolved, particularly when children are involved. Some of the issues which divorcing couples seek to resolve by mediation include the division of property accumulated during the marriage; spousal maintenance; child support; and child custody and visitation.

In litigation, the parties are often advised to take an adversarial position on the issues, rather than encouraged to compromise, despite the obvious disadvantages. Divorce and custody litigation is time consuming and expensive, and the court calendars are backlogged. When a stalemate occurs, the most private of matters—such as the ownership of one's personal property or the custody of, and visitation with, one's child—are ultimately decided by a stranger to the marriage.

The ensuing legal battle exacts an enormous emotional toll on all of the parties, particularly the children, who often feel that they are somehow to blame when their parents decide to separate. They experience feelings of guilt as they attempt to satisfy their need for the love and nurturing of both parents, while feeling the pressure of having to "choose sides." Children—even at a very young age—are quite aware of their parents' emotional state, no matter how hard the adults attempt to hide their anger and bitterness. The adversarial nature of protracted litigation necessarily exacerbates the hostility. Thus, the children are likely to experience greater psychological trauma over an extended period of time, particularly when they are directly inserted into the litigation as bargaining chips.

DIVORCE AND CUSTODY MEDIATION

Mediation in the area of divorce and family relations is emerging as a viable alternative to litigation, particularly by couples who are concerned with maintaining any kind of amicable relationship with their former spouse. This is crucial when children are involved, because the parties will necessarily have some degree of contact with each other following the divorce. Many couples prefer to mediate their divorce out of a sense of responsibility to the psychological and emotional well-being of their children. Mediation attempts to reduce the animosity, and resolve issues in a cooperative and communicative atmosphere, with the best interests of the children as the paramount concern.

Mediation helps in maintaining a civil relationship between the divorcing couple because it takes the decision making out of the hands of third parties, and places this responsibility on the parties themselves. This gives the divorcing couple a sense of control over their situation, unlike litigation which basically reduces the litigants to silent observers using lawyers as their mouthpieces.

Most divorcing couples are primarily interested in working out a fair and equitable resolution of the issues. This is the goal of divorce mediation, however, both parties must be willing participants for mediation to succeed. If either of the parties has a "winner/loser" attitude, their only option is litigation. Divorce mediation seeks to make both parties "winners" in the sense that they reach a fair settlement of the issues of the divorce, maintain civility in their relationship, and avoid draining their respective bank accounts.

As with mediation in general, divorce mediation is carried out using the services of a professional divorce mediator. Again, it is important to choose the most effective and experienced mediator for your particular situation, in order to achieve a successful result. As noted above, professional mediators are often experienced and educated in the areas of psychology or sociology. This experience is particularly useful in the context of a divorce, an intensely emotional event. Professional divorce mediators also have varying degrees of expertise in the substantive matters of divorce, such as the financial and legal issues and, if those issues fall outside of their expertise, they should instruct their clients to seek outside professional assistance early on in the process.

Finally, it should be pointed out that only a court of law with proper jurisdiction can legally dissolve a marriage. Nevertheless, once the issues have been worked out between the couple through successful mediation, and an agreement has been formalized, the substance of that agreement need only be submitted to the judge for inclusion in the divorce decree—a ministerial act. The underlying divorce action is usually filed as an uncontested no-fault divorce, or separation agreement in contemplation of divorce in the few jurisdictions which do not yet permit "no-fault" divorce.

APPENDIX 1:
NATIONAL DIRECTORY OF DISPUTE RESOLUTION SERVICES

STATE	ORGANIZATION	ADDRESS	TELEPHONE NUMBER
ALABAMA	BETTER BUSINESS BUREAU, INC.	1214 SOUTH 20TH STREET BIRMINGHAM AL 35202	205-933-2893
ALASKA	BETTER BUSINESS BUREAU OF ALASKA	3380 C STREET SUITE 103 ANCHORAGE AK 99503	907-562-2824
ARIZONA	COMMUNITY MEDIATION PROGRAM	PO BOX 26504 TUCSON, AZ 85726	602-323-1706
ARKANSAS	ARKANSAS CONSUMER PROTECTION PROGRAM	400 TOWER BUILDING FOURTH AND CENTER STREETS LITTLE ROCK, AR 72201	501-682-2341

STATE	ORGANIZATION	ADDRESS	TELEPHONE NUMBER
CALIFORNIA	LOS ANGELES COUNTY BAR ASSOCIATION DISPUTE RESOLUTION SERVICE	617 SOUTH OLIVE STREET LOS ANGELES, CA 90014	213-627-2727
CALIFORNIA	STATE DEPARTMENT OF CONSUMER AFFAIRS CONSUMER ASSISTANCE OFFICE	1020 N STREET ROOM 500 SACRAMENTO, CA 95818	916-445-1254
CALIFORNIA	CALIFORNIA COMMUNITY DISPUTE SERVICES	445 BUSH STREET 5TH FLOOR SAN FRANCISCO, CA 94108	415-434-2200
COLORADO	OFFICE OF CONSUMER PROTECTION	1525 SHERMAN STREET ROOM 215 DENVER, CO 80203	303-866-5168
CONNECTICUT	WATERBURY SUPERIOR COURT MEDIATION PROGRAM	28 GRAND STREET HARTFORD, CT 06106	860-566-8187
DELAWARE	MEDIATION UNIT OF THE DELAWARE FAMILY COURT	PO BOX 2359 WILMINGTON, DE 19899	302-571-2270
DISTRICT OF COLUMBIA	CIVIL ARBITRATION PROGRAM D.C. SUPERIOR COURT CIVIL DIVISION	500 INDIANA AVENUE, NW WASHINGTON, DC 20001	202-879-1680
DISTRICT OF COLUMBIA	FEDERAL MEDIATION AND CONCILIATION SERVICE	2100 K STREET, NW WASHINGTON, DC 20427	202-653-5300
FLORIDA	METRO MEDIATION SERVICES	1500 NW 12TH AVENUE ROOM 708 MIAMI, FL 33126	305-547-7885

STATE	ORGANIZATION	ADDRESS	TELEPHONE NUMBER
GEORGIA	GOVERNOR'S OFFICE OF CONSUMER AFFAIRS	TWO MARTIN LUTHER KING DRIVE SUITE 356, EAST TOWER ATLANTA, GA 30334	404-656-1760
HAWAII	PROGRAM ON ALTERNATIVE DISPUTE RESOLUTION	PO BOX 2560 HONOLULU, HI 96804	808-548-3080
IDAHO	IDAHO HUMAN RIGHTS COMMISSION	450 WEST STATE STREET BOISE, ID 83720	208-334-2873
ILLINOIS	ILLINOIS CONSUMER PROTECTION DIVISION	500 SOUTH SECOND SPRINGFIELD, IL 62706	217-782-9011
INDIANA	INDIANA CONSUMER PROTECTION DIVISION	219 STATE HOUSE INDIANAPOLIS, IN 46204	317-232-6203
IOWA	IOWA ATTORNEY GENERAL'S OFFICE	1300 EAST WALNUT DES MOINES, IA 50319	515-281-5926
KANSAS	DISPUTE RESOLUTION SERVICES	465 SOUTH PARKER SUITE 103 OLATHE, KS 66061	913-764-8585
KENTUCKY	PRETRIAL SERVICES	514 WEST LIBERTY STREET SUITE 105 LOUISVILLE, KY 40212	502-588-4142
LOUISIANA	BETTER BUSINESS BUREAU	1401 NORTH MARKET STREET SHREVEPORT, LA 71107	318-221-8352

STATE	ORGANIZATION	ADDRESS	TELEPHONE NUMBER
MAINE	COURT MEDIATION SERVICE	PO BOX 66, D.T.S PORTLAND, ME 04112	207-879-4700
MARYLAND	MARYLAND CONSUMER-BUSINESS BINDING ARBITRATION PROGRAM	138 EAST ANTIETAM STREET SUITE 210 HAGERSTOWN, MD 21740	301-791-4780
MARYLAND	U.S. DEPARTMENT OF JUSTICE COMMUNITY RELATIONS SERVICE,	5550 FRIENDSHIP BOULEVARD SUITE 330 CHEVY CHASE, MD 20815	301-492-5948
MASSACHUSETTS	FACE-TO-FACE MEDIATION PROGRAM	131 TREMONT STREET BOSTON, MA 02111	617-727-2200
MASSACHUSETTS	MASSACHUSETTS BOARD OF CONCILIATION AND ARBITRATION	100 CAMBRIDGE STREET ROOM 1105 BOSTON, MA 02202	617-727-3466
MICHIGAN	CONSUMER PROTECTION DIVISION	690 LAW BUILDING 525 WEST OTTAWA STREET LANSING, MI 48913	517-373-1140
MINNESOTA	ACROSS THE BOARD MEDIATION/ARBITRATION AND BETTER BUSINESS BUREAU AUTOLINE PROGRAM	2706 GANNON ROAD ST. PAUL, MN 55116	612-646-4637
MINNESOTA	CONSUMER SERVICES DIVISION	117 UNIVERSITY AVENUE ROOM 124 ST. PAUL, MN 55155	612-296-3353

STATE	ORGANIZATION	ADDRESS	TELEPHONE NUMBER
MISSISSIPPI	BETTER BUSINESS BUREAU OF MISSISSIPPI	510 GEORGE STREET SUITE 107 JACKSON, MS 39202	601-948-8222
MISSOURI	BETTER BUSINESS BUREAU OF SOUTHWEST MISSOURI	205 PARK CENTRAL EAST SUITE 509 SPRINGFIELD, MO 65806	417-862-9231
NEBRASKA	BETTER BUSINESS BUREAU	719 NORTH 48TH STREET LINCOLN, NB 68504	402-467-5261
NEVADA	DIVISION OF CONSUMER AFFAIRS	2601 EAST SAHARA AVENUE SUITE 247 LAS VEGAS, NV 89104	702-386-5293
NEW HAMPSHIRE	NEW HAMPSHIRE MEDIATION PROGRAM	33 STICKNEY AVENUE CONCORD, NH 03301	603-224-8043
NEW JERSEY	OFFICE OF CONSUMER PROTECTION	1100 RAYMOND BOULEVARD NEWARK, NJ 07102	201-648-3622
NEW JERSEY	CENTER FOR PUBLIC DISPUTE RESOLUTION	RICHARD J. HUGHES JUSTICE COMPLEX 25 MARKET STREET, CN 850 TRENTON, NJ 08625	609-292-1773
NEW MEXICO	NEW MEXICO CENTER FOR DISPUTE RESOLUTION	510 SECOND STREET, NW SUITE 209 ALBUQUERQUE, NM 87102	505-247-0571

STATE	ORGANIZATION	ADDRESS	TELEPHONE NUMBER
NEW YORK	COMMUNITY DISPUTE RESOLUTION CENTER	ALFRED E. SMITH BUILDING FIRST FLOOR ALBANY, NY 12225	518-473-4160
NEW YORK	CITY OF NEW YORK DEPARTMENT OF CONSUMER AFFAIRS	80 LAFAYETTE STREET NEW YORK, NY 10013	212-577-0111
NORTH CAROLINA	DISPUTE SETTLEMENT CENTER OF DURHAM INC.	PO BOX 2321 DURHAM, NC 27702	919-490-6777
NORTH DAKOTA	FEE ARBITRATION PANEL	PO BOX 2136 BISMARCK, ND 58502	701-255-1404
OHIO	BETTER BUSINESS BUREAU	425 JEFFERSON AVENUE TOLEDO, OH 43604	419-241-6276
OHIO	COMMUNITY MEDIATION SERVICES OF CENTRAL OHIO	2504 SULLIVAN AVENUE COLUMBUS, OH 43204	614-276-7837
OKLAHOMA	EARLY SETTLEMENT PROGRAM	600 CIVIC CENTER ROOM 134 TULSA, OK 74103	918-596-7786
OREGON	NEIGHBORHOOD MEDIATION CENTER	4815 N.E. SEVENTH AVENUE PORTLAND, OR 97211	503-243-7320
PENNSYLVANIA	DISPUTE RESOLUTION PROGRAM	PHILADELPHIA MUNICIPAL COURT CITY HALL ANNEX ROOM 1005 PHILADELPHIA, PA 19107	215-686-2973

STATE	ORGANIZATION	ADDRESS	TELEPHONE NUMBER
PENNSYLVANIA	PITTSBURGH MEDIATION CENTER	7101 HAMILTON AVENUE PITTSBURGH, PA 15208	412-371-1231
RHODE ISLAND	BETTER BUSINESS BUREAU OF RHODE ISLAND INC.	100 BIGNALL STREET WARWICK, RI 02887	
SOUTH CAROLINA	OFFICE OF EXECUTIVE POLICY AND PROGRAMS	1205 PENDLETON STREET COLUMBIA, SC 29201	803-734-0457
SOUTH DAKOTA	DIVISION OF CONSUMER AFFAIRS STATE CAPITOL BUILDING	500 EAST CAPITOL PIERRE, SD 57501	605-773-4400
TENNESSEE	TENNESSEE DIVISION OF CONSUMER AFFAIRS	500 JAMES ROBERTSON PARKWAY FIFTH FLOOR NASHVILLE, TN 37219	615-741-4737
TEXAS	DISPUTE MEDIATION SERVICE OF DALLAS INC.	3310 LIVE OAK SUITE 202-LB9 DALLAS, TX 75204	214-754-0022
TEXAS	DISPUTE RESOLUTION CENTER	301 SAN JACINTO SUITE 315 HOUSTON, TX 77001	713-221-6222
UTAH	DIVISION OF CONSUMER PROTECTION	160 EAST 300 SOUTH SALT LAKE CITY, UT 84145	801-530-6601
VERMONT	DISPUTE RESOLUTION CLINIC OF WOODBURY COLLEGE	659 ELM STREET MONTPELIER, VT 05602	802-229-0516

STATE	ORGANIZATION	ADDRESS	TELEPHONE NUMBER
VIRGINIA	DISPUTE RESOLUTION CENTER	701 EAST FRANKLIN STREET SUITE 712 RICHMOND, VA 23219	804-343-7355
WASHINGTON	BETTER BUSINESS BUREAU OF WASHINGTON	333 S.W. FIFTH AVENUE PORTLAND, OR 97204	503-226-3981
WISCONSIN	OFFICE OF CONSUMER PROTECTION	123 WEST WASHINGTON AVENUE ROOM 170 MADISON, WI 53707	608-266-1852
WYOMING	BETTER BUSINESS BUREAU	2144 SAGE AVENUE CASPER, WY 82604	307-268-2616

Note: This directory contains the larger state-wide dispute resolution programs handling a variety of types of cases in each state listed. There are many smaller dispute resolution programs conducted by various organizations serving specified geographical regions and more particularized caseloads within each state. For a more detailed list please consult the source.*

* Source: Dispute Resolution Program Directory, American Bar Association, 750 N. Lake Shore Drive, Chicago, IL 60611 (Tel): 312-988-5000/(Fax): 312-988-5568

APPENDIX 2:
DIRECTORY OF INTERNATIONAL
ARBITRATION AGENCIES

COUNTRY	ADDRESS
AUSTRALIA	Australian Centre for International Commercial Arbitration 6th Floor Building B World Trade Centre Melbourne Victoria 3005
AUSTRALIA	Australian Commercial Disputes Centre Level 21 Remington Centre 175 Liverpool Street Sydney NSW 2000
AUSTRIA	Arbitral Centre of the Federal Economic Chamber Vienna Wiedner Haupstrabe 63 P.O. Box 190 A-1045 Vienna
BELGIUM	Belgian Center for the Study and the Practice of National and International Arbitration (CEPANI)8 Rue des Sols 1000 Brussels
BULGARIA	Bulgarian Chamber of Commerce and Industry Court of Arbitration 11-A Stamboliisky Boulevard Sofia
CANADA	Arbitrators' Institute of Canada 234 Eglinton Avenue East Suite 411 Toronto Ontario M4P 1K5
CANADA	British Columbia International Commercial Arbitration Centre 670-999 Canada Place Vancouver, British Columbia V6C 2E2

COUNTRY	ADDRESS
CANADA	Canadian Arbitration Conciliation and Amicable Composition Centre University of Ottawa Ottawa
CANADA	Quebec National and International Commercia Arbitration Centre Edifice la Laurentienne 500 Grande-Allee Est Rez-de-Chaussee, Quebec, PQ G1R 2J7
CHINA	China International Economic and Trade Arbitration Commission 1 Fu Xing Men Wai Street Beijing
CHINA	China Maritime Arbitration Commission 1 Fu Xing Men Wai Street Beijing
DENMARK	Danish Institute of Arbitration Frederiksborggade 1
EGYPT	Regional Centre for Commercial Arbitration at Cairo 3 Abu el-Feda Street Zamalek, Cairo
FINLAND	Central Chamber of Commerce of Finland Board of Arbitration Fabianinkatu 14B P.O. Box 1000 00101 Helsinki
FRANCE	French Arbitration Association 2 Rue de Harley 75001 Paris
GERMANY	German Arbitration Institute P.O. Box 100 447 Kolumbastrabe 5 D-5000 Koln 1
GREECE	Greek Arbitration Association 102 Solonos Street Athens 10680
HONG KONG	Hong Kong International Arbitration Centre 1 Arbuthnot Road Central
HUNGARY	Hungarian Chamber of Commerce Arbitration Court Kossuth Lajoster 6-8 1389 Budapest V
INDIA	Indian Council of Arbitration Federation House Tansen Marg New Delhi 110001
INDONESIA	Indonesian National Arbitration Board Jalan Merdek Timur 11 Jakarta

COUNTRY	ADDRESS
INTER-AMERICA	Inter-American Commercial Arbitration Commission 1889 F Street NW Room 760-D S. 400-D Washington, DC 20006
INTERNATIONAL	International Centre for Settlement of Investment Disputes 1818 H Street NW Washington, DC 20433
INTERNATIONAL	ICC International Court of Arbitration 38 Cours Albert 1er 5008 Paris
INTERNATIONAL	International Federation of Commercial Arbitration Associations c/o American Arbitration Association 140 West 51st Street New York, NY 10020-1203
ITALY	Italian Arbitration Association 5 Via XX Settembre 00187 Roma
JAPAN	Japan Commercial Arbitration Association Izumi Shibakoen Building 608 Shibakoen 1-chome Minato-ku Tokyo
KOREA	Korean Commercial Arbitration Board 43rd Floor Trade Tower 159 Samsung-Dong Kangnam-ku CPO Box 50 Seoul 135-729
MALAYSIA	Regional Centre for Arbitration at Kuala Lumpur 576 Jalan Sultan Salahuddin 50480 Kuala Lumpur
THE NETHERLANDS	Netherlands Arbitration Institute Schouwburgplein 30-34 P.O. Box 22105 3003 DC Rotterdam
NEW ZEALAND	Arbitrators' Institute of New Zealand 16 Palmer Street P.O. Box 1477 Wellington
PAKISTAN	Federation of Pakistan Chambers of Commerce and Industry Commercial Arbitration Tribunal Share-a-Firdousi Main Clifton Karachi-6
POLAND	International Court of Arbitration for Marine and Inland Navigation Gydnia Ul. Pulaskiego 6 81-368 Gdynia

COUNTRY	ADDRESS
POLAND	Polish Chamber of Foreign Trade Arbitration Court Trebacka 4 P.O. Box 361 00-074 Warsaw
RUSSIA	Chamber of Commerce and Industry Foreign Trade Arbitration Commission 6 Kuibyshev Street 101000 Moscow
SCOTLAND	Scottish Council for Arbitration 55 Queen Street Edinburgh EH2 3PA
SINGAPORE	Singapore Institute of Arbitrators c/o Singapore Professional Centre 129-B Blk.23 Outram Park 0316
SPAIN	Spanish Arbitration Association Plaza San Amaro 1 Madrid 20
SWEDEN	Stockholm Chamber of Commerce Arbitration Institute P.O. Box 16050 S-103-22 Stockholm 16
SWITZERLAND	Chamber of Commerce of Basel St. Alban-Graben 8 4001 Basel
SWITZERLAND	Berne Chamber of Commerce Gutenbergstrabe 1 PO Box 5464 3011 Berne
SWITZERLAND	Chamber of Commerce of Zurich Bleicherweg 5 P.O. Box 4031 8022 Zurich
SWITZERLAND	Geneva Chamber of Commerce and Industry 4 Boulevard du Theatre 1211 Geneva 11
TAIWAN	Commercial Arbitration Association of the Republic of China 390 Fuhsing South Road, Sec. 1 6th Floor Taipei
UNITED KINGDOM	London Court of International Arbitration 30-32 St. Mary Axe London EC3A 8ET
UNITED STATES	American Arbitration Association International Center for Dispute Resolution 1622 Broadway New York, NY 10019-6708

Source: Business Arbitration: What you Need to Know, American Arbitration Association 1991.

APPENDIX 3:
NATIONAL DIRECTORY OF AMERICAN ARBITRATION ASSOCIATION (AAA) OFFICES

STATE	ADDRESS	TELEPHONE NUMBER	FAX NUMBER
ARIZONA	333 EAST OSBORN ROAD SUITE 310 PHOENIX AZ 85012-2365	602-234-0950	602-230-2151
CALIFORNIA	2030 MAIN STREET SUITE 1650 IRVINE, CA 92614-7240	949-251-9840	949-251-9842

STATE	ADDRESS	TELEPHONE NUMBER	FAX NUMBER
CALIFORNIA	3055 WILSHIRE BOULEVARD FLOOR 7 LOS ANGELES, CA 90010-1108	213-383-6516	213-386-2251
CALIFORNIA	600 B STREET SUITE 1450 SAN DIEGO, CA 92101-4586	619-239-3051	619-239-3807
CALIFORNIA	225 BUSH STREET FLOOR 18 SAN FRANCISCO, CA 94104-4207	415-981-3901	415-781-8426
COLORADO	1660 LINCOLN STREET SUITE 2150 DENVER, CO 80264-2101	303-831-0823	303-832-3626
CONNECTICUT	111 FOUNDERS PLAZA FLOOR 17 EAST HARTFORD, CT 06108-3240	860-289-3993	860-282-0459
DISTRICT OF COLUMBIA	601 PENNSYLVANIA AVENUE N.W SUITE 700 WASHINGTON, DC 20004-2676	202-737-9191	202-737-9099
FLORIDA	799 BRICKELL PLAZA SUITE 600 MIAMI, FL 33131-2808	305-358-7777	305-358-4931

STATE	ADDRESS	TELEPHONE NUMBER	FAX NUMBER
FLORIDA	315 EAST ROBINSON STREET SUITE 290 ORLANDO, FL 32801-2742	407-648-1185	407-649-8668
GEORGIA	2200 CENTURY PARKWAY SUITE 300 ATLANTA, GA 30345-3203	404-325-0101	404-325-8034
ILLINOIS	225 NORTH MICHIGAN AVENUE SUITE 2527 CHICAGO, IL 60601-7601	312-616-6560	312-819-0404
LOUISIANA	2810 ENERGY CENTRE 1100 POYDRAS STREET NEW ORLEANS, LA 70163-2810	504-522-8781	504-561-8041
MASSACHUSETTS	133 FEDERAL STREET FLOOR 10 BOSTON, MA 02110-1703	617-451-6600	617-451-0763
MICHIGAN	ONE TOWNE SQUARE SUITE 1600 SOUTHFIELD, MI 48076-3728	248-352-5500	248-352-3147
MINNESOTA	700 PILLSBURY CENTER 200 SOUTH SIXTH STREET MINNEAPOLIS, MN 55402-1092	612-332-6545	612-342-2334

STATE	ADDRESS	TELEPHONE NUMBER	FAX NUMBER
MISSOURI	1101 WALNUT STREET SUITE 903 KANSAS CITY, MO 64106-2110	816-221-6401	816-471-5264
MISSOURI	ONE MERCANTILE CENTER SUITE 2512 ST. LOUIS, MO 63101-1614	314-621-7175	314-621-3730
NEVADA	5440 WEST SAHARA AVENUE SUITE 206 LAS VEGAS, NV 89146-0365	702-252-4071	702-252-4073
NEW JERSEY	265 DAVIDSON AVENUE SUITE 140 SOMERSET, NJ 08873-4159	732-560-9560	732-560-8850
NEW YORK (CORPORATE HEADQUARTERS)	335 MADISON AVENUE FLOOR 10 NEW YORK, NY 10017-4605	212-716-5800	212-716-5905
NEW YORK (INTERNATIONAL CENTER FOR DISPUTE RESOLUTION)	1633 BROADWAY FLOOR 10 NEW YORK, NY 10019-6708	212-484-4181	212-246-7274
NEW YORK	666 OLD COUNTRY ROAD SUITE 603 GARDEN CITY, NY 11530-2004	516-222-1660	516-745-6447
NEW YORK	140 WEST 51ST STREET NEW YORK, NY 10020-1203	212-484-4000	212-307-4387

STATE	ADDRESS	TELEPHONE NUMBER	FAX NUMBER
NEW YORK	65 BROADWAY NEW YORK, NY 10006	917-438-1500	917-438-1600
NEW YORK	115 EAST JEFFERSON STREET SUITE 401 SYRACUSE, NY 13202-2595	315-472-5483	315-472-0966
NEW YORK	399 KNOLLWOOD ROAD SUITE 116 WHITE PLAINS, NY 10603-1916	914-946-1119	914-946-2661
NORTH CAROLINA	6100 FAIRVIEW ROAD SUITE 300 CHARLOTTE, NC 28210-3277	704-347-0200	704-347-2804
OHIO	525 VINE STREET SUITE 1070 CINCINNATI, OH 45202-3123	513-241-8434	513-241-8437
OHIO	25050 COUNTRY CLUB BOULEVARD SUITE 200 NORTH OLMSTED, OH 44070	440-716-2220	440-716-2221
PENNSYLVANIA	230 SOUTH BROAD STREET FLOOR 12 PHILADELPHIA, PA 19102-4199	215-732-5260	215-732-5002
PENNSYLVANIA	FOUR GATEWAY CENTER ROOM 1939 PITTSBURGH, PA 15222-1207	412-261-3617	412-261-6055

STATE	ADDRESS	TELEPHONE NUMBER	FAX NUMBER
TENNESSEE	211 SEVENTH AVENUE NORTH SUITE 300 NASHVILLE, TN 37219-1823	615-256-5857	615-244-8570
TEXAS	1750 TWO GALLERIA TOWER 13455 NOEL ROAD DALLAS, TX 75240-6636	972-702-8222	972-490-9008
TEXAS	1001 FANNIN STREET SUITE 1005 HOUSTON, TX 77002-6708	713-739-1302	713-739-1702
UTAH	645 SOUTH 200TH STREET EAST SUITE 203 SALT LAKE CITY, UT 84111-3834	801-531-9748	801-323-9624
VIRGINIA	707 EAST MAIN STREET SUITE 1610 RICHMOND, VA 23219-2803	804-649-4838	804-698-7365
WASHINGTON	1020 ONE UNION SQUARE 600 UNIVERSITY STREET SEATTLE, WA 98101-4111	206-622-6435	206-343-5679

Source: American Arbitration Association 2000.

APPENDIX 4:
THE CODE OF ETHICS FOR ARBITRATORS
IN COMMERCIAL DISPUTES

Canon I. An Arbitrator Should Uphold the Integrity and Fairness of the Arbitration Process.

A. Fair and just processes for resolving disputes are indispensable in our society. Commercial arbitration is an important method for deciding many types of disputes. In order for commercial arbitration to be effective, there must be broad public confidence in the integrity and fairness of the process. Therefore, an arbitrator has a responsibility not only to the parties but also to the process of arbitration itself, and must observe high standards of conduct so that the integrity and fairness of the process will be preserved. Accordingly, an arbitrator should recognize a responsibility to the public, to the parties whose rights will be decided, and to all other participants in the proceeding. The provisions of this code should be construed and applied to further these objectives.

B. It is inconsistent with the integrity of the arbitration process for persons to solicit appointment for themselves. However, a person may indicate a general willingness to serve as an arbitrator.

C. Persons should accept appointment as arbitrators only if they believe that they can be available to conduct the arbitration promptly.

D. After accepting appointment and while serving as an arbitrator, a person should avoid entering into any financial, business, professional, family or social relationship, or acquiring any financial or personal interest, which is likely to affect impartiality or which might reasonably create the appearance of partiality or bias. For a reasonable period of time after the decision of a case, persons who have served as arbitrators should avoid entering into any such relationship, or acquiring any such interest, in circumstances which might reasonably create the appearance that they had been influenced in the arbitration by the anticipation or expectation of the relationship or interest.

E. Arbitrators should conduct themselves in a way that is fair to all parties and should not be swayed by outside pressure, by public clamor, by fear of criticism or by self-interest.

F. When an arbitrator's authority is derived from an agreement of the parties, the arbitrator should neither exceed that authority nor do less than is required to exercise that authority completely. Where the agreement of the parties sets forth procedures to be followed in conducting the arbitration or refers to rules to be followed, it is the obligation of the arbitrator to comply with such procedures or rules.

G. An arbitrator should make all reasonable efforts to prevent delaying tactics, harassment of parties or other participants, or other abuse or disruption of the arbitration process.

H. The ethical obligations of an arbitrator begin upon acceptance of the appointment and continue throughout all stages of the proceeding. In addition, wherever specifically set forth in this code, certain ethical obligations begin as soon as a person is requested to serve as an arbitrator and certain ethical obligations continue even after the decision in the case has been given to the parties.

Canon II. An Arbitrator Should Disclose Any Interest or Relationship Likely to Affect Impartiality or Which Might Create an Appearance of Partiality or Bias.

Introductory Note

This code reflects the prevailing principle that arbitrators should disclose the existence of interests or relationships that are likely to affect their impartiality or that might reasonably create an appearance that they are biased against one party or favorable to another. These provisions of the code are intended to be applied realistically so that the burden of detailed disclosure does not become so great that it is impractical for persons in the business world to be arbitrators, thereby depriving parties of the services of those who might be best informed and qualified to decide particular types of case. See Footnote.

This code does not limit the freedom of parties to agree on whomever they choose as an arbitrator. When parties, with knowledge of a person's interests and relationships, nevertheless desire that individual to serve as an arbitrator, that person may properly serve.

A. Persons who are requested to serve as arbitrators should, before accepting, disclose

1. any direct or indirect financial or personal interest in the outcome of the arbitration;

2. any existing or past financial, business, professional, family or social relationships which are likely to affect impartiality or which might reasonably create an appearance of partiality or bias. Persons requested to serve as arbitrators should disclose any such relationships which they personally have with any party or its lawyer, or with any individual whom they have been told will be a witness. They should also disclose any such relationships involving members of their families or their current employers, partners or business associates.

B. Persons who are requested to accept appointment as arbitrators should make a reasonable effort to inform themselves of any interests or relationships described in the preceding paragraph A.

C. The obligation to disclose interests or relationships described in the preceding paragraph A is a continuing duty which requires a person who accepts appointment as an arbitrator to disclose, at any stage of the arbitration, any such interests or relationships which may arise, or which are recalled or discovered.

D. Disclosure should be made to all parties unless other procedures for disclosure are provided in the rules or practices of an institution which is administering the arbitration. Where more than one arbitrator has been appointed, each should inform the others of the interests and relationships which have been disclosed.

E. In the event that an arbitrator is requested by all parties to withdraw, the arbitrator should do so. In the event that an arbitrator is requested to withdraw by less than all of the parties because of alleged partiality or bias, the arbitrator should withdraw unless either of the following circumstances exists.

1. If an agreement of the parties, or arbitration rules agreed to by the parties, establishes procedures for determining challenges to arbitrators, then those procedures should be followed; or,

2. if the arbitrator, after carefully considering the matter, determines that the reason for the challenge is not substantial, and that he or she can nevertheless act and decide the case impartially and fairly, and that withdrawal would cause unfair delay or expense to another party or would be contrary to the ends of justice.

Canon III. An Arbitrator in Communicating with the Parties Should Avoid Impropriety or the Appearance of Impropriety.

A. If an agreement of the parties or applicable arbitration rules referred to in that agreement, establishes the manner or content of communications between the arbitrator and the parties, the arbitrator should follow those procedures notwithstanding any contrary provision of the following paragraphs B and C.

B. Unless otherwise provided in applicable arbitration rules or in an agreement of the parties, arbitrators should not discuss a case with any party in the absence of each other party, except in any of the following circumstances.

1. Discussions may be had with a party concerning such matters as setting the time and place of hearings or making other arrangements for the conduct of the proceedings. However, the arbitrator should promptly inform each other party of the discussion and should not make any final determination concerning the matter discussed before giving each absent party an opportunity to express its views.

2. If a party fails to be present at a hearing after having been given due notice, the arbitrator may discuss the case with any party who is present.

3. If all parties request or consent to it, such discussion may take place.

C. Unless otherwise provided in applicable arbitration rules or in an agreement of the parties, whenever an arbitrator communicates in writing with one party, the arbitrator should at the same time send a copy of the communication to each other party. Whenever the arbitrator receives any written communication concerning the case from one party which has not already been sent to each other party, the arbitrator should do so.

Canon IV. An Arbitrator Should Conduct The Proceedings Fairly And Diligently.

A. An arbitrator should conduct the proceedings in an evenhanded manner and treat all parties with equality and fairness at all stages of the proceedings.

B. An arbitrator should perform duties diligently and conclude the case as promptly as the circumstances reasonably permit.

C. An arbitrator should be patient and courteous to the parties, to their lawyers and to the witnesses and should encourage similar conduct by all participants in the proceedings.

D. Unless otherwise agreed by the parties or provided in arbitration rules agreed to by the parties, an arbitrator should accord to all parties the right to appear in person and to be heard after due notice of the time and place of hearing.

E. An arbitrator should not deny any party the opportunity to be represented by counsel.

F. If a party fails to appear after due notice, an arbitrator should proceed with the arbitration when authorized to do so by the agreement of the parties, the rules agreed to by the parties or by law. However, an arbitrator should do so only after receiving assurance that notice has been given to the absent party.

G. When an arbitrator determines that more information than has been presented by the parties is required to decide the case, it is not improper for the arbitrator to ask questions, call witnesses, and request documents or other evidence.

H. It is not improper for an arbitrator to suggest to the parties that they discuss the possibility of settlement of the case. However, an arbitrator should not be present or otherwise participate in the settlement discussions unless requested to do so by all parties. An arbitrator should not exert pressure on any party to settle.

I. Nothing in this code is intended to prevent a person from acting as a mediator or conciliator of a dispute in which he or she has been appointed as arbitrator, if requested to do so by all parties or where authorized or required to do so by applicable laws or rules.

J. When there is more than one arbitrator, the arbitrators should afford each other the full opportunity to participate in all aspects of the proceedings.

Canon V. An Arbitrator Should Make Decisions in a Just, Independent And Deliberate Manner.

A. An arbitrator should, after careful deliberation, decide all issues submitted for determination. An arbitrator should decide no other issues.

B. An arbitrator should decide all matters justly, exercising independent judgment, and should not permit outside pressure to affect the decision.

C. An arbitrator should not delegate the duty to decide to any other person.

D. In the event that all parties agree upon a settlement of issues in dispute and request an arbitrator to embody that agreement in an award, an arbitrator may do so, but is not required to do so unless satisfied with the propriety of the terms of settlement. Whenever an arbitrator embodies a settlement by the parties in an award, the arbitrator should state in the award that it is based on an agreement of the parties.

Canon VI. An Arbitrator Should Be Faithful to The Relationship of Trust And Confidentiality Inherent in That Office.

A. An arbitrator is in a relationship of trust to the parties and should not, at any time, use confidential information acquired during the arbitration proceeding to gain personal advantage or advantage for others, or to affect adversely the interest of another.

B. Unless otherwise agreed by the parties, or required by applicable rules or law, an arbitrator should keep confidential all matters relating to the arbitration proceedings and decision.

C. It is not proper at any time for an arbitrator to inform anyone of the decision in advance of the time it is given to all parties. In a case in which there is more than one arbitrator, it is not proper at any time for an arbitrator to inform anyone concerning the deliberations of the arbitrators. After an arbitration award has been made, it is not proper for an arbitrator to assist in post-arbitral proceedings, except as is required by law.

D. In many types of arbitration it is customary practice for the arbitrators to serve without pay. However, in some types of cases it is customary for arbitrators to receive compensation for their services and reimbursement for their expenses. In cases in which any such payments are to be made, all persons who are requested to serve, or who are serving as arbitrators, should be governed by the same high standards of integrity and fairness as apply to their other activities in the case. Accordingly, such persons should scrupulously avoid bargaining with parties over the amount of payments or engaging in any communications concerning payments which would create an appearance of coercion or other impropriety. In the absence of governing provisions in the agreement of the parties or in rules agreed to by the parties or in applicable law, certain practices relating to payments are generally recognized as being preferable in order to preserve the integrity and fairness of the arbitration process. These practices include the following.

1. It is preferable that before the arbitrator finally accepts appointment the basis of payment be established and that all parties be informed thereof in writing.

2. In cases conducted under the rules or administration of an institution that is available to assist in making arrangements for payments, the payments should be arranged by the institution to avoid the neces-

sity for communication by the arbitrators directly with the parties concerning the subject.

3. In cases where no institution is available to assist in making arrangement for payments, it is preferable that any discussions with arbitrators concerning payments should take place in the presence of all parties.

Canon VII. Ethical Considerations Relating to Arbitrators Appointed by One Party

Introductory Note

In some types of arbitration in which there are three arbitrators, it is customary for each party, acting alone, to appoint one arbitrator. The third arbitrator is then appointed by agreement either of the parties or of the two arbitrators, or, failing such agreement, by an independent institution or individual. In some of these types of arbitration, all three arbitrators are customarily considered to be neutral and are expected to observe the same standards of ethical conduct. However, there are also many types of tripartite arbitration in which it has been the practice that the two arbitrators appointed by the parties are not considered to be neutral and are expected to observe many but not all of the same ethical standards as the neutral third arbitrator. For the purposes of this code, an arbitrator appointed by one party who is not expected to observe all of the same standards as the third arbitrator is called a "nonneutral arbitrator." This Canon VII describes the ethical obligations that nonneutral party-appointed arbitrators should observe and those that are not applicable to them.

In all arbitrations in which there are two or more party-appointed arbitrators, it is important for everyone concerned to know from the start whether the party-appointed arbitrators are expected to be neutrals or nonneutrals. In such arbitrations, the two party-appointed arbitrators should be considered nonneutrals unless both parties inform the arbitrators that all three arbitrators are to be neutral or unless the contract, the applicable arbitration rules, or any governing law requires that all three arbitrators be neutral.

It should be noted that, in cases conducted outside the United States, the applicable law might require that all arbitrators be neutral. Accordingly, in such cases, the governing law should be considered before applying any of the following provisions relating to nonneutral party-appointed arbitrators.

FOOTNOTES

A. *Obligations under Canon I*

Nonneutral party-appointed arbitrators should observe all of the obligations of Canon I to uphold the integrity and fairness of the arbitration process, subject only to the following provisions.

1. Nonneutral arbitrators may be predisposed toward the party who appointed them but in all other respects are obligated to act in good faith and with integrity and fairness. For example, nonneutral arbitrators should not engage in delaying tactics or harassment of any party or witness and should not knowingly make untrue or misleading statements to the other arbitrators.

2. The provisions of Canon I.D relating to relationships and interests are not applicable to nonneutral arbitrators.

B. *Obligations under Canon II*

Nonneutral party-appointed arbitrators should disclose to all parties, and to the other arbitrators, all interests and relationships which Canon II requires be disclosed. Disclosure as required by Canon II is for the benefit not only of the party who appointed the nonneutral arbitrator, but also for the benefit of the other parties and arbitrators so that they may know of any bias which may exist or appear to exist. However, this obligation is subject to the following provisions.

1. Disclosure by nonneutral arbitrators should be sufficient to describe the general nature and scope of any interest or relationship, but need not include as detailed information as is expected from persons appointed as neutral arbitrators.

2. Nonneutral arbitrators are not obliged to withdraw if requested to do so by the party who did not appoint them, notwithstanding the provisions of Canon II.E.

C. *Obligations under Canon III*

Nonneutral party-appointed arbitrators should observe all of the obligations of Canon III concerning communications with the parties, subject only to the following provisions.

1. In an arbitration in which the two party-appointed arbitrators are expected to appoint the third arbitrator, nonneutral arbitrators may consult with the party who appointed them concerning the acceptability of persons under consideration for appointment as the third arbitrator.

2. Nonneutral arbitrators may communicate with the party who appointed them concerning any other aspect of the case, provided they first inform the other arbitrators and the parties that they intend to do so. If such communication occurred prior to the time the person was appointed as arbitrator, or prior to the first hearing or other meeting of the parties with the arbitrators, the nonneutral arbitrator should, at the first hearing or meeting, disclose the fact that such communication has taken place. In complying with the provisions of this paragraph, it is sufficient that there be disclosure of the fact that such communication has occurred without disclosing the content of the communication. It is also sufficient to disclose at any time the intention to follow the procedure of having such communications in the future and there is no requirement thereafter that there be disclosure before each separate occasion on which such a communication occurs.

3. When nonneutral arbitrators communicate in writing with the party who appointed them concerning any matter as to which communication is permitted under this code, they are not required to send copies of any such written communication to any other party or arbitrator.

D. Obligations under Canon IV

Nonneutral party-appointed arbitrators should observe all of the obligations of Canon IV to conduct the proceedings fairly and diligently.

E. Obligations under Canon V

Nonneutral party-appointed arbitrators should observe all of the obligations of Canon V concerning making decisions, subject only to the following provision.

1. Nonneutral arbitrators are permitted to be predisposed toward deciding in favor of the party who appointed them.

F. Obligations under Canon VI

Nonneutral party-appointed arbitrators should observe all of the obligations of Canon VI to be faithful to the relationship of trust inherent in the office of arbitrator, subject only to the following provision.

1. Nonneutral arbitrators are not subject to the provisions of Canon VI.D with respect to any payments by the party who appointed them.*

---

*   Source: American Arbitration Association, 1999.

APPENDIX 5:
MODEL STANDARDS OF CONDUCT FOR MEDIATORS

I. Self-Determination: A Mediator shall Recognize that Mediation is Based on the Principle of Self-Determination by the Parties.

Self-determination is the fundamental principle of mediation. It requires that the mediation process rely upon the ability of the parties to reach a voluntary, uncoerced agreement. Any party may withdraw from mediation at any time.

COMMENTS

1. The mediator may provide information about the process, raise issues, and help parties explore options. The primary role of the mediator is to facilitate a voluntary resolution of a dispute. Parties shall be given the opportunity to consider all proposed options.

2. A mediator cannot personally ensure that each party has made a fully informed choice to reach a particular agreement, but is a good practice for the mediator to make the parties aware of the importance of consulting other professionals, where appropriate, to help them make informed decisions.

II. Impartiality: A Mediator shall Conduct the Mediation in an Impartial Manner.

The concept of mediator impartiality is central to the mediation process. A mediator shall mediate only those matters in which she or he can remain impartial and evenhanded. If at any time the mediator is unable to conduct the process in an impartial manner, the mediator is obligated to withdraw.

COMMENTS

1. A mediator shall avoid conduct that gives the appearance of partiality toward one of the parties. The quality of the mediation process is enhanced when the parties have confidence in the impartiality of the mediator.

2. When mediators are appointed by a court or institution, the appointing agency shall make reasonable efforts to ensure that mediators serve impartially.

3. A mediator should guard against partiality or prejudice based on the parties' personal characteristics, background or performance at the mediation.

III. Conflicts of Interest: A Mediator shall Disclose all Actual and Potential Conflicts of Interest Reasonably Known to the Mediator. After Disclosure, the Mediator shall Decline to Mediate unless all Parties Choose to Retain the Mediator. The Need to Protect Against Conflicts of Interest also Governs Conduct that Occurs During and After the Mediation.

A conflict of interest is a dealing or relationship that might create an impression of possible bias. The basic approach to questions of conflict of interest is consistent with the concept of self-determination. The mediator has a responsibility to disclose all actual and potential conflicts that are reasonably known to the mediator and could reasonably be seen as raising a question about impartiality. If all parties agree to mediate after being informed of conflicts, the mediator may proceed with the mediation. If, however, the conflict of interest casts serious doubt on the integrity of the process, the mediator shall decline to proceed.

A mediator must avoid the appearance of conflict of interest both during and after the mediation. Without the consent of all parties, a mediator shall not subsequently establish a professional relationship with one of the parties in a related matter, or in an unrelated matter under circumstances which would raise legitimate questions about the integrity of the mediation process.

COMMENTS

1. A mediator shall avoid conflicts of interest in recommending the services of other professionals. A mediator may make reference to professional referral services or associations which maintain rosters of qualified professionals.

2. Potential conflicts of interest may arise between administrators of mediation programs and mediators and there may be strong pressures on the mediator to settle a particular case or cases. The mediator's commitment must be to the parties and the process. Pressure from outside of the mediation process should never influence the mediator to coerce parties to settle.

IV. Competence: A Mediator shall Mediate Only When the Mediator has the Necessary Qualifications to Satisfy the Reasonable Expectations of the Parties.

Any person may be selected as a mediator, provided that the parties are satisfied with the mediator's qualifications. Training and experience in mediation, however, are often necessary for effective mediation. A person who offers herself or himself as available to serve as a mediator gives parties and the public the expectation that she or he has the competency to mediate effectively. In court-connected or other forms of mandated mediation, it is essential that mediators assigned to the parties have the requisite training and experience.

COMMENTS

1. Mediators should have information available for the parties regarding their relevant training, education and experience.

2. The requirements for appearing on the list of mediators must be made public and available to interested persons.

3. When mediators are appointed by a court or institution, the appointing agency shall make reasonable efforts to ensure that each mediator is qualified for the particular mediation.

V. Confidentiality: A Mediator shall Maintain the Reasonable Expectations of the Parties with Regard to Confidentiality.

The reasonable expectations of the parties with regard to confidentiality shall be met by the mediator. The parties' expectations of confidentiality depend on the circumstances of the mediation and any agreements they may make. The mediator shall not disclose any matter that a party expects to be confidential unless given permission by all parties or unless required by law or other public policy.

COMMENTS

1. The parties may make their own rules with respect to confidentiality, or other accepted practice of an individual mediator or institution may dictate a particular set of expectations. Since the parties' expectations

regarding confidentiality are important, the mediator should discuss these expectations with the parties.

2. If the mediator holds private sessions with a party, the nature of these sessions with regard to confidentiality should be discussed prior to undertaking such sessions.

3. In order to protect the integrity of the mediation, a mediator should avoid communicating information about how the parties acted in the mediation process, the merits of the case, or settlement offers. The mediator may report, if required, whether parties appeared at a scheduled mediation.

4. Where the parties have agreed that all or a portion of the information disclosed during a mediation is confidential, the parties' agreement should be respected by the mediator.

5. Confidentiality should not be construed to limit or prohibit the effective monitoring, research, or evaluation of mediation programs by responsible persons. Under appropriate circumstances, researchers may be permitted to obtain access to the statistical data and, with the permission of the parties, to individual case files, observations of live mediations, and interviews with participants.

VI. Quality of the Process: A Mediator shall Conduct the Mediation Fairly, Diligently, and in a Manner Consistent with the Principle of Self-Determination by the Parties.

A mediator shall work to ensure a quality process and to encourage mutual respect among the parties. A quality process requires a commitment by the mediator to diligence and procedural fairness. There should be adequate opportunity for each party in the mediation to participate in the discussions. The parties decide when and under what conditions they will reach an agreement or terminate a mediation.

COMMENTS

1. A mediator may agree to mediate only when he or she is prepared to commit the attention essential to an effective mediation.

2. Mediators should only accept cases when they can satisfy the reasonable expectations of the parties concerning the timing of the process. A mediator should not allow a mediation to be unduly delayed by the parties or their representatives.

3. The presence or absence of persons at a mediation depends on the agreement of the parties and the mediator. The parties and mediator

may agree that others may be excluded from particular sessions or from the entire mediation process.

4. The primary purpose of a mediator is to facilitate the parties' voluntary agreement. This role differs substantially from other professional-client relationships. Mixing the role of a mediator and the role of a professional advising a client is problematic, and mediators must strive to distinguish between the roles. A mediator should, therefore, refrain from providing professional advice. Where appropriate, a mediator should recommend that parties seek outside professional advice, or consider resolving their dispute through arbitration, counseling, neutral evaluation, or other processes. A mediator who undertakes, at the request of the parties, an additional dispute resolution role in the same matter assumes increased responsibilities and obligations that may be governed by the standards of other processes.

5. A mediator shall withdraw from a mediation when incapable of serving or when unable to remain impartial.

6. A mediator shall withdraw from a mediation or postpone a session if the mediation is being used to further illegal conduct, or if a party is unable to participate due to drug, alcohol, or other physical or mental incapacity.

7. Mediators should not permit their behavior in the mediation process to be guided by a desire for a high settlement rate.

VII. Advertising and Solicitation: A Mediator shall be Truthful in Advertising and Solicitation for Mediation.

Advertising or any other communication with the public concerning services offered or regarding the education, training, and expertise of the mediator shall be truthful. Mediators shall refrain from promises and guarantees of results.

COMMENTS

1. It is imperative that communication with the public educate and instill confidence in the process.

2. In an advertisement or other communication to the public, a mediator may make reference to meeting state, national, or private organization qualifications only if the entity referred to has a procedure for qualifying mediators and the mediator has been duly granted the requisite status.

VIII. Fees: A Mediator shall fully Disclose and Explain the Basis of Compensation, Fees, and Charges to the Parties.

The parties should be provided sufficient information about fees at the outset of a mediation to determine if they wish to retain the services of a mediator. If a mediator charges fees, the fees shall be reasonable, considering among other things, the mediation service, the type and complexity of the matter, the expertise of the mediator, the time required, and the rates customary in the community. The better practice in reaching an understanding about fees is to set down the arrangements in a written agreement.

COMMENTS

1. A mediator who withdraws from a mediation should return any unearned fee to the parties.

2. A mediator should not enter into a fee agreement which is contingent upon the result of the mediation or amount of the settlement.

3. Co-mediators who share a fee should hold to standards of reasonableness in determining the allocation of fees.

4. A mediator should not accept a fee for referral of a matter to another mediator or to any other person.

IX. Obligations to the Mediation Process: Mediators have a Duty to Improve the Practice of Mediation.

COMMENT

1. Mediators are regarded as knowledgeable in the process of mediation. They have an obligation to use their knowledge to help educate the public about mediation; to make mediation accessible to those who would like to use it; to correct abuses; and to improve their professional skills and abilities.*

---

*   Source: American Arbitration Association, 1999.

APPENDIX 6:
ADMINISTRATIVE DISPUTE RESOLUTION ACT OF 1996 (5 U.S.C. 571 ET SEQ)— SELECTED PROVISIONS

Subchapter IV—Alternative Means of Dispute Resolution In the Administrative Process

5 U.S.C. § 571. Definitions

For the purposes of this subchapter, the term—

(1) "agency" has the same meaning as in section 551(1) of this title;

(2) "administrative program" includes a Federal function which involves protection of the public interest and the determination of rights, privileges, and obligations of private persons through rule making, adjudication, licensing, or investigation, as those terms are used in subchapter II of this chapter;

(3) "alternative means of dispute resolution" means any procedure that is used to resolve issues in controversy, including, but not limited to, conciliation, facilitation, mediation, factfinding, minitrials, arbitration, and use of ombuds, or any combination thereof;

(4) "award" means any decision by an arbitrator resolving the issues in controversy;

(5) "dispute resolution communication" means any oral or written communication prepared for the purposes of a dispute resolution proceeding, including any memoranda, notes or work product of the neutral, parties or nonparty participant; except that a written agreement to enter into a dispute resolution proceeding, or final written agreement

or arbitral award reached as a result of a dispute resolution proceeding, is not a dispute resolution communication;

(6) "dispute resolution proceeding" means any process in which an alternative means of dispute resolution is used to resolve an issue in controversy in which a neutral is appointed and specified parties participate;

(7) "in confidence" means, with respect to information, that the information is provided—

(A) with the expressed intent of the source that it not be disclosed; or

(B) under circumstances that would create the reasonable expectation on behalf of the source that the information will not be disclosed;

(8) "issue in controversy" means an issue which is material to a decision concerning an administrative program of an agency, and with which there is disagreement—

(A) between an agency and persons who would be substantially affected by the decision; or

(B) between persons who would be substantially affected by the decision;

(9) "neutral" means an individual who, with respect to an issue in controversy, functions specifically to aid the parties in resolving the controversy;

(10) "party" means—

(A) for a proceeding with named parties, the same as in section 551(3) of this title; and

(B) for a proceeding without named parties, a person who will be significantly affected by the decision in the proceeding and who participates in the proceeding;

(11) "person" has the same meaning as in section 551(2) of this title; and

(12) "roster" means a list of persons qualified to provide services as neutrals.

SHORT TITLE

This Act . . . May be cited as the "Administrative Dispute Resolution Act."

CONGRESSIONAL FINDINGS

Section 2 of Pub. L. 101-552 provided that: "The Congress finds that—

"(1) administrative procedure, as embodied in chapter 5 of title 5, United States Code, and other statutes, is intended to offer a prompt, expert, and inexpensive means of resolving disputes as an alternative to litigation in the Federal courts;

"(2) administrative proceedings have become increasingly formal, costly, and lengthy resulting in unnecessary expenditures of time and in a decreased likelihood of achieving consensual resolution of disputes;

"(3) alternative means of dispute resolution have been used in the private sector for many years and, in appropriate circumstances, have yielded decisions that are faster, less expensive, and less contentious;

"(4) such alternative means can lead to more creative, efficient, and sensible outcomes;

"(5) such alternative means may be used advantageously in a wide variety of administrative programs;

"(6) explicit authorization of the use of well-tested dispute resolution techniques will eliminate ambiguity of agency authority under existing law;

"(7) Federal agencies may not only receive the benefit of techniques that were developed in the private sector, but may also take the lead in the further development and refinement of such techniques; and

"(8) the availability of a wide range of dispute resolution procedures, and an increased understanding of the most effective use of such procedures, will enhance the operation of the Government and better serve the public."

PROMOTION OF ALTERNATIVE MEANS OF DISPUTE RESOLUTION

Section 3 of Pub. L. 101-552, as amended Pub. L. 104-320, Sec.4(a), Oct. 19, 1996, 110 Stat. 3871, provided that:

"(a) Promulgation of Agency Policy.—Each agency shall adopt a policy that addresses the use of alternative means of dispute resolution and case management. In developing such a policy, each agency shall—

"(1) consult with the agency designated by, or the interagency committee designated or established by, the President under section 573 of title 5, United States Code, to facilitate and encourage agency use of alternative dispute resolution under subchapter IV of chapter 5 of such title; and

"(2) examine alternative means of resolving disputes in connection with—

"(A) formal and informal adjudications;

"(B) rulemakings;

"(C) enforcement actions;

"(D) issuing and revoking licenses or permits;

"(E) contract administration;

"(F) litigation brought by or against the agency; and

"(G) other agency actions.

"(b) Dispute Resolution Specialists.—The head of each agency shall designate a senior official to be the dispute resolution specialist of the agency. Such official shall be responsible for the implementation of—

"(1) the provisions of this Act [see Short Title note above] and the amendments made by this Act; and

"(2) the agency policy developed under subsection (a).

"(c) Training.—Each agency shall provide for training on a regular basis for the dispute resolution specialist of the agency and other employees involved in implementing the policy of the agency developed under subsection (a). Such training should encompass the theory and practice of negotiation, mediation, arbitration, or related techniques. The dispute resolution specialist shall periodically recommend to the agency head agency employees who would benefit from similar training.

"(d) Procedures for Grants and Contracts.—

"(1) Each agency shall review each of its standard agreements for contracts, grants, and other assistance and shall determine whether to amend any such standard agreements to authorize and encourage the use of alternative means of dispute resolution.

"(2)(A) Within 1 year after the date of the enactment of this Act (Nov. 15, 1990), the Federal Acquisition Regulation shall be amended, as necessary, to carry out this Act (see Short Title note above) and the amendments made by this Act.

"(B) For purposes of this section, the term 'Federal Acquisition Regulation' means the single system of Government-wide procurement regulation referred to in section 6(a) of the Office of Federal Procurement Policy Act (41 U.S.C. § 405(a))."

USE OF NONATTORNEYS

Section 9 of Pub. L. 101-552 provided that:

"(a) Representation of Parties.—Each agency, in developing a policy on the use of alternative means of dispute resolution under this Act (see Short Title note above), shall develop a policy with regard to the representation by persons other than attorneys of parties in alternative dispute resolution proceedings and shall identify any of its administrative programs with numerous claims or disputes before the agency and determine—

"(1) the extent to which individuals are represented or assisted by attorneys or by persons who are not attorneys; and

"(2) whether the subject areas of the applicable proceedings or the procedures are so complex or specialized that only attorneys may adequately provide such representation or assistance.

"(b) Representation and Assistance by Nonattorneys.—A person who is not an attorney may provide representation or assistance to any individual in a claim or dispute with an agency, if—

"(1) such claim or dispute concerns an administrative program identified under subsection (a);

"(2) such agency determines that the proceeding or procedure does not necessitate representation or assistance by an attorney under subsection (a)(2); and

"(3) such person meets any requirement of the agency to provide representation or assistance in such a claim or dispute.

"(c) Disqualification of Representation or Assistance.—Any agency that adopts regulations under subchapter IV of chapter 5 of title 5, United States Code, to permit representation or assistance by persons who are not attorneys shall review the rules of practice before such agency to—

"(1) ensure that any rules pertaining to disqualification of attorneys from practicing before the agency shall also apply, as appropriate, to other persons who provide representation or assistance; and

"(2) establish effective agency procedures for enforcing such rules of practice and for receiving complaints from affected persons."

5 U.S.C. § 572. General authority

(a) An agency may use a dispute resolution proceeding for the resolution of an issue in controversy that relates to an administrative program, if the parties agree to such proceeding.

(b) An agency shall consider not using a dispute resolution proceeding if—

(1) a definitive or authoritative resolution of the matter is required for precedential value, and such a proceeding is not likely to be accepted generally as an authoritative precedent;

(2) the matter involves or may bear upon significant questions of Government policy that require additional procedures before a final resolution may be made, and such a proceeding would not likely serve to develop a recommended policy for the agency;

(3) maintaining established policies is of special importance, so that variations among individual decisions are not increased and such a proceeding would not likely reach consistent results among individual decisions;

(4) the matter significantly affects persons or organizations who are not parties to the proceeding;

(5) a full public record of the proceeding is important, and a dispute resolution proceeding cannot provide such a record; and

(6) the agency must maintain continuing jurisdiction over the matter with authority to alter the disposition of the matter in the light of changed circumstances, and a dispute resolution proceeding would interfere with the agency's fulfilling that requirement.

(c) Alternative means of dispute resolution authorized under this subchapter are voluntary procedures which supplement rather than limit other available agency dispute resolution techniques.

5 U.S.C. § 573. Neutrals

(a) A neutral may be a permanent or temporary officer or employee of the Federal Government or any other individual who is acceptable to the parties to a dispute resolution proceeding. A neutral shall have no official, financial, or personal conflict of interest with respect to the issues in controversy, unless such interest is fully disclosed in writing to all parties and all parties agree that the neutral may serve.

(b) A neutral who serves as a conciliator, facilitator, or mediator serves at the will of the parties.

(c) The President shall designate an agency or designate or establish an interagency committee to facilitate and encourage agency use of dispute resolution under this subchapter. Such agency or interagency committee, in consultation with other appropriate Federal agencies and professional organizations experienced in matters concerning dispute resolution, shall—

(1) encourage and facilitate agency use of alternative means of dispute resolution; and

(2) develop procedures that permit agencies to obtain the services of neutrals on an expedited basis.

(d) An agency may use the services of one or more employees of other agencies to serve as neutrals in dispute resolution proceedings. The agencies may enter into an interagency agreement that provides for the reimbursement by the user agency or the parties of the full or partial cost of the services of such an employee.

(e) Any agency may enter into a contract with any person for services as a neutral, or for training in connection with alternative means of dispute resolution. The parties in a dispute resolution proceeding shall agree on compensation for the neutral that is fair and reasonable to the Government.

5 U.S.C. § 574. Confidentiality

(a) Except as provided in subsections (d) and (e), a neutral in a dispute resolution proceeding shall not voluntarily disclose or through discovery or compulsory process be required to disclose any dispute resolution communication or any communication provided in confidence to the neutral, unless—

(1) all parties to the dispute resolution proceeding and the neutral consent in writing, and, if the dispute resolution communication was provided by a nonparty participant, that participant also consents in writing;

(2) the dispute resolution communication has already been made public;

(3) the dispute resolution communication is required by statute to be made public, but a neutral should make such communication public only if no other person is reasonably available to disclose the communication; or

(4) a court determines that such testimony or disclosure is necessary to—

(A) prevent a manifest injustice;

(B) help establish a violation of law; or

(C) prevent harm to the public health or safety, of sufficient magnitude in the particular case to outweigh the integrity of dispute resolution proceedings in general by reducing the confidence of parties in future cases that their communications will remain confidential.

(b) A party to a dispute resolution proceeding shall not voluntarily disclose or through discovery or compulsory process be required to disclose any dispute resolution communication, unless—

(1) the communication was prepared by the party seeking disclosure;

(2) all parties to the dispute resolution proceeding consent in writing;

(3) the dispute resolution communication has already been made public;

(4) the dispute resolution communication is required by statute to be made public;

(5) a court determines that such testimony or disclosure is necessary to—

(A) prevent a manifest injustice;

(B) help establish a violation of law; or

(C) prevent harm to the public health and safety, of sufficient magnitude in the particular case to outweigh the integrity of dispute resolution proceedings in general by reducing the confidence of parties in future cases that their communications will remain confidential;

(6) the dispute resolution communication is relevant to determining the existence or meaning of an agreement or award that resulted from the dispute resolution proceeding or to the enforcement of such an agreement or award; or

(7) except for dispute resolution communications generated by the neutral, the dispute resolution communication was provided to or was available to all parties to the dispute resolution proceeding.

(c) Any dispute resolution communication that is disclosed in violation of subsection (a) or (b), shall not be admissible in any proceeding relating to the issues in controversy with respect to which the communication was made.

(d)(1)The parties may agree to alternative confidential procedures for disclosures by a neutral. Upon such agreement the parties shall inform the neutral before the commencement of the dispute resolution proceeding of any modifications to the provisions of subsection (a) that will govern the confidentiality of the dispute resolution proceeding. If the parties do not so inform the neutral, subsection (a) shall apply.

(2) To qualify for the exemption established under subsection (j), an alternative confidential procedure under this subsection may not provide for less disclosure than the confidential procedures otherwise provided under this section.

(e) If a demand for disclosure, by way of discovery request or other legal process, is made upon a neutral regarding a dispute resolution communication, the neutral shall make reasonable efforts to notify the parties and any affected nonparty participants of the demand. Any party or affected nonparty participant who receives such notice and within 15 calendar days does not offer to defend a refusal of the neutral to disclose the requested information shall have waived any objection to such disclosure.

(f) Nothing in this section shall prevent the discovery or admissibility of any evidence that is otherwise discoverable, merely because the evidence was presented in the course of a dispute resolution proceeding.

(g) Subsections (a) and (b) shall have no effect on the information and data that are necessary to document an agreement reached or order issued pursuant to a dispute resolution proceeding.

(h) Subsections (a) and (b) shall not prevent the gathering of information for research or educational purposes, in cooperation with other agencies, governmental entities, or dispute resolution programs, so long as the parties and the specific issues in controversy are not identifiable.

(i) Subsections (a) and (b) shall not prevent use of a dispute resolution communication to resolve a dispute between the neutral in a dispute resolution proceeding and a party to or participant in such proceeding, so long as such dispute resolution communication is disclosed only to the extent necessary to resolve such dispute.

(j) A dispute resolution communication which is between a neutral and a party and which may not be disclosed under this section shall also be exempt from disclosure under section 552(b)(3).

5 U.S.C. § 575. Authorization of arbitration

(a)(1) Arbitration may be used as an alternative means of dispute resolution whenever all parties consent. Consent may be obtained either before or after an issue in controversy has arisen. A party may agree to—

(A) submit only certain issues in controversy to arbitration; or

(B) arbitration on the condition that the award must be within a range of possible outcomes.

(2) The arbitration agreement that sets forth the subject matter submitted to the arbitrator shall be in writing. Each such arbitration agreement shall specify a maximum award that may be issued by the arbitrator and may specify other conditions limiting the range of possible outcomes.

(3) An agency may not require any person to consent to arbitration as a condition of entering into a contract or obtaining a benefit.

(b) An officer or employee of an agency shall not offer to use arbitration for the resolution of issues in controversy unless such officer or employee—

(1) would otherwise have authority to enter into a settlement concerning the matter; or

(2) is otherwise specifically authorized by the agency to consent to the use of arbitration.

(c) Prior to using binding arbitration under this subchapter, the head of an agency, in consultation with the Attorney General and after taking into account the factors in section 572(b), shall issue guidance on the appropriate use of binding arbitration and when an officer or employee of the agency has authority to settle an issue in controversy through binding arbitration.

5 U.S.C. § 576. Enforcement of arbitration agreements

An agreement to arbitrate a matter to which this subchapter applies is enforceable pursuant to section 4 of title 9, and no action brought to enforce such an agreement shall be dismissed nor shall relief therein be denied on the grounds that it is against the United States or that the United States is an indispensable party.

5 U.S.C. § 577. Arbitrators

(a) The parties to an arbitration proceeding shall be entitled to participate in the selection of the arbitrator.

(b) The arbitrator shall be a neutral who meets the criteria of section 573 of this title.

5 U.S.C. § 578. Authority of the arbitrator

An arbitrator to whom a dispute is referred under this subchapter may—

(1) regulate the course of and conduct arbitral hearings;

(2) administer oaths and affirmations;

(3) compel the attendance of witnesses and production of evidence at the hearing under the provisions of section 7 of title 9 only to the extent the agency involved is otherwise authorized by law to do so; and

(4) make awards.

5 U.S.C. § 579. Arbitration proceedings

(a) The arbitrator shall set a time and place for the hearing on the dispute and shall notify the parties not less than 5 days before the hearing.

(b) Any party wishing a record of the hearing shall—

(1) be responsible for the preparation of such record;

(2) notify the other parties and the arbitrator of the preparation of such record;

(3) furnish copies to all identified parties and the arbitrator; and

(4) pay all costs for such record, unless the parties agree otherwise or the arbitrator determines that the costs should be apportioned.

(c)(1) The parties to the arbitration are entitled to be heard, to present evidence material to the controversy, and to cross-examine witnesses appearing at the hearing.

(2) The arbitrator may, with the consent of the parties, conduct all or part of the hearing by telephone, television, computer, or other electronic means, if each party has an opportunity to participate.

(3) The hearing shall be conducted expeditiously and in an informal manner.

(4) The arbitrator may receive any oral or documentary evidence, except that irrelevant, immaterial, unduly repetitious, or privileged evidence may be excluded by the arbitrator.

(5) The arbitrator shall interpret and apply relevant statutory and regulatory requirements, legal precedents, and policy directives.

(d) No interested person shall make or knowingly cause to be made to the arbitrator an unauthorized ex parte communication relevant to the merits of the proceeding, unless the parties agree otherwise. If a communication is made in violation of this subsection, the arbitrator shall ensure that a memorandum of the communication is prepared and made a part of the record, and that an opportunity for rebuttal is allowed. Upon receipt of a communication made in violation of this subsection, the arbitrator may, to the extent consistent with the interests of justice and the policies underlying this subchapter, require the offending party to show cause why the claim of such party should not be resolved against such party as a result of the improper conduct.

(e) The arbitrator shall make the award within 30 days after the close of the hearing, or the date of the filing of any briefs authorized by the arbitrator, whichever date is later, unless—

(1) the parties agree to some other time limit; or

(2) the agency provides by rule for some other time limit.

5 U.S.C. § 580. Arbitration awards

(a)(1) Unless the agency provides otherwise by rule, the award in an arbitration proceeding under this subchapter shall include a brief, informal discussion of the factual and legal basis for the award, but formal findings of fact or conclusions of law shall not be required.

(2) The prevailing parties shall file the award with all relevant agencies, along with proof of service on all parties.

(b) The award in an arbitration proceeding shall become final 30 days after it is served on all parties. Any agency that is a party to the proceeding may extend this 30-day period for an additional 30-day period by serving a notice of such extension on all other parties before the end of the first 30-day period.

(c) A final award is binding on the parties to the arbitration proceeding, and may be enforced pursuant to sections 9 through 13 of title 9. No action brought to enforce such an award shall be dismissed nor shall relief therein be denied on the grounds that it is against the United States or that the United States is an indispensable party.

(d) An award entered under this subchapter in an arbitration proceeding may not serve as an estoppel in any other proceeding for any issue that was resolved in the proceeding. Such an award also may not be used as precedent or otherwise be considered in any factually unrelated proceeding, whether conducted under this subchapter, by an agency, or in a court, or in any other arbitration proceeding.

5 U.S.C. § 581. Judicial Review

(a) Notwithstanding any other provision of law, any person adversely affected or aggrieved by an award made in an arbitration proceeding conducted under this subchapter may bring an action for review of such award only pursuant to the provisions of sections 9 through 13 of title 9.

(b) A decision by an agency to use or not to use a dispute resolution proceeding under this subchapter shall be committed to the discretion of the agency and shall not be subject to judicial review, except that arbitration shall be subject to judicial review under section 10(b) of title 9.

APPENDIX 7:
THE FEDERAL ARBITRATION ACT
(9 U.S.C. §1 ET SEQ)—SELECTED
PROVISIONS

Chapter 1. General Provisions

Section 1. "Maritime transactions" and "commerce" defined; exceptions to operation of title

"Maritime transaction", as herein defined, means charter parties, bills of lading of water carriers, agreements relating to wharfage, supplies furnished vessels or repairs to vessels, collisions, or any other matters in foreign commerce which, if the subject of controversy, would be embraced within admiralty jurisdiction; "commerce", as herein defined, means commerce among the several States or with foreign nations, or in any Territory of the United States or in the District of Columbia, or between any such Territory and another, or between any such Territory and any State or foreign nation, or between the District of Columbia and any State or Territory or foreign nation, but nothing herein contained shall apply to contracts of employment of seamen, railroad employees, or any other class of workers engaged in foreign or interstate commerce.

Section 2. Validity, irrevocability, and enforcement of agreements to arbitrate

A written provision in any maritime transaction or a contract evidencing a transaction involving commerce to settle by arbitration a controversy thereafter arising out of such contract or transaction, or the refusal to perform the whole or any part thereof, or an agreement in writing to submit to arbitration an existing controversy arising out of such a contract, transaction, or refusal, shall be valid, irrevocable, and enforceable, save upon such grounds as exist at law or in equity for the revocation of any contract.

Section 3. Stay of proceedings where issue therein referable to arbitration

If any suit or proceeding be brought in any of the courts of the United States upon any issue referable to arbitration under an agreement in writing for such arbitration, the court in which such suit is pending, upon being satisfied that the issue involved in such suit or proceeding is referable to arbitration under such an agreement, shall on application of one of the parties stay the trial of the action until such arbitration has been had in accordance with the terms of the agreement, providing the applicant for the stay is not in default in proceeding with such arbitration.

Section 4. Failure to arbitrate under agreement; petition to United States court having jurisdiction for order to compel arbitration; notice and service thereof; hearing and determination

A party aggrieved by the alleged failure, neglect, or refusal of another to arbitrate under a written agreement for arbitration may petition any United States district court which, save for such agreement, would have jurisdiction under Title 28, in a civil action or in admiralty of the subject matter of a suit arising out of the controversy between the parties, for an order directing that such arbitration proceed in the manner provided for in such agreement. Five days' notice in writing of such application shall be served upon the party in default. Service thereof shall be made in the manner provided by the Federal Rules of Civil Procedure. The court shall hear the parties, and upon being satisfied that the making of the agreement for arbitration or the failure to comply therewith is not in issue, the court shall make an order directing the parties to proceed to arbitration in accordance with the terms of the agreement. The hearing and proceedings, under such agreement, shall be within the district in which the petition for an order directing such arbitration is filed. If the making of the arbitration agreement or the failure, neglect, or refusal to perform the same be in issue, the court shall proceed summarily to the trial thereof. If no jury trial be demanded by the party alleged to be in default, or if the matter in dispute is within admiralty jurisdiction, the court shall hear and determine such issue. Where such an issue is raised, the party alleged to be in default may, except in cases of admiralty, on or before the return day of the notice of application, demand a jury trial of such issue, and upon such demand the court shall make an order referring the issue or issues to a jury in the manner provided by the Federal Rules of Civil Procedure, or may specially call a jury for that purpose. If the jury find that no agreement in writing for arbitration was made or that there is no default in proceeding thereunder, the proceeding shall be dismissed. If the jury find that an agreement for arbitration was made in writing and that there is a default in proceeding thereunder, the court shall make an order summarily directing the parties to proceed with the arbitration in accordance with the terms thereof.

Section 5. Appointment of arbitrators or umpire

If in the agreement provision be made for a method of naming or appointing an arbitrator or arbitrators or an umpire, such method shall be followed; but if no method be provided therein, or if a method be provided and any party thereto shall fail to avail himself of such method, or if for any other reason there shall be a lapse in the naming of an arbitrator or arbitrators or umpire, or in filling a vacancy, then upon the application of either party to the controversy the court shall designate and appoint an arbitrator or arbitrators or umpire, as the case may require, who shall act under the said agreement with the same force and effect as if he or they had been specifically named therein; and unless otherwise provided in the agreement the arbitration shall be by a single arbitrator.

Section 6. Application heard as motion

Any application to the court hereunder shall be made and heard in the manner provided by law for the making and hearing of motions, except as otherwise herein expressly provided.

Section 7. Witnesses before arbitrators; fees; compelling attendance

The arbitrators selected either as prescribed in this title or otherwise, or a majority of them, may summon in writing any person to attend before them or any of them as a witness and in a proper case to bring with him or them any book, record, document, or paper which may be deemed material as evidence in the case. The fees for such attendance shall be the same as the fees of witnesses before masters of the United States courts. Said summons shall issue in the name of the arbitrator or arbitrators, or a majority of them, and shall be signed by the arbitrators, or a majority of them, and shall be directed to the said person and shall be served in the same manner as subpoenas to appear and testify before the court; if any person or persons so summoned to testify shall refuse or neglect to obey said summons, upon petition the United States district court for the district in which such arbitrators, or a majority of them, are sitting may compel the attendance of such person or persons before said arbitrator or arbitrators, or punish said person or persons for contempt in the same manner provided by law for securing the attendance of witnesses or their punishment for neglect or refusal to attend in the courts of the United States.

Section 8. Proceedings begun by libel in admiralty and seizure of vessel or property

If the basis of jurisdiction be a cause of action otherwise justiciable in admiralty, then, notwithstanding anything herein to the contrary, the party claiming to be aggrieved may begin his proceeding hereunder by seizure of the vessel or other property of the other party according to the usual course of admiralty proceedings, and the court shall then have jurisdiction to direct the parties to proceed with the arbitration and shall retain jurisdiction to enter its decree upon the award.

Section 9. Award of arbitrators; confirmation; jurisdiction; procedure

If the parties in their agreement have agreed that a judgment of the court shall be entered upon the award made pursuant to the arbitration, and shall specify the court, then at any time within one year after the award is made any party to the arbitration may apply to the court so specified for an order confirming the award, and thereupon the court must grant such an order unless the award is vacated, modified, or corrected as prescribed in sections 10 and 11 of this title. If no court is specified in the agreement of the parties, then such application may be made to the United States court in and for the district within which such award was made. Notice of the application shall be served upon the adverse party, and thereupon the court shall have jurisdiction of such party as though he had appeared generally in the proceeding. If the adverse party is a resident of the district within which the award was made, such service shall be made upon the adverse party or his attorney as prescribed by law for service of notice of motion in an action in the same court. If the adverse party shall be a nonresident, then the notice of the application shall be served by the marshal of any district within which the adverse party may be found in like manner as other process of the court.

Section 10. Same; vacation; grounds; rehearing

a. In any of the following cases the United States court in and for the district wherein the award was made may make an order vacating the award upon the application of any party to the arbitration

1. Where the award was procured by corruption, fraud, or undue means.

2. Where there was evident partiality or corruption in the arbitrators, or either of them.

3. Where the arbitrators were guilty of misconduct in refusing to postpone the hearing, upon sufficient cause shown, or in refusing to hear

evidence pertinent and material to the controversy; or of any other misbehavior by which the rights of any party have been prejudiced.

4. Where the arbitrators exceeded their powers, or so imperfectly executed them that a mutual, final, and definite award upon the subject matter submitted was not made.

5. Where an award is vacated and the time within which the agreement required the award to be made has not expired the court may, in its discretion, direct a rehearing by the arbitrators.

b. The United States district court for the district wherein an award was made that was issued pursuant to section 590 of title 5 may make an order vacating the award upon the application of a person, other than a party to the arbitration, who is adversely affected or aggrieved by the award, if the use of arbitration or the award is clearly inconsistent with the factors set forth in section 582 of title 5.

Section 11. Same; modification or correction; grounds; order In either of the following cases the United States court in and for the district wherein the award was made may make an order modifying or correcting the award upon the application of any party to the arbitration—

a. Where there was an evident material miscalculation of figures or an evident material mistake in the description of any person, thing, or property referred to in the award.

b. Where the arbitrators have awarded upon a matter not submitted to them, unless it is a matter not affecting the merits of the decision upon the matter submitted.

c. Where the award is imperfect in matter of form not affecting the merits of the controversy.

The order may modify and correct the award, so as to effect the intent thereof and promote justice between the parties.

Section 12. Notice of motions to vacate or modify; service; stay of proceedings

Notice of a motion to vacate, modify, or correct an award must be served upon the adverse party or his attorney within three months after the award is filed or delivered. If the adverse party is a resident of the district within which the award was made, such service shall be made upon the adverse party or his attorney as prescribed by law for service of notice of motion in an action in the same court. If the adverse party shall be a nonresident then the notice of the application shall be served by the marshal of any district within which the adverse party may be found in like manner as other process of the court. For the purposes of the motion any judge who might make an order to stay the proceedings in an action brought in the same court may make an order, to be served with the notice of motion, staying the proceedings of the adverse party to enforce the award.

Section 13. Papers filed with order on motions; judgment; docketing; force and effect; enforcement

The party moving for an order confirming, modifying, or correcting an award shall, at the time such order is filed with the clerk for the entry of judgment thereon, also file the following papers with the clerk:

a. The agreement; the selection or appointment, if any, of an additional arbitrator or umpire; and each written extension of the time, if any, within which to make the award.

b. The award.

c. Each notice, affidavit, or other paper used upon an application to confirm, modify, or correct the award, and a copy of each order of the court upon such an application.

The judgment shall be docketed as if it was rendered in an action. The judgment so entered shall have the same force and effect, in all respects, as, and be subject to all the provisions of law relating to, a judgment in an action; and it may be enforced as if it had been rendered in an action in the court in which it is entered.

Section 14. Contracts not affected

This title shall not apply to contracts made prior to January 1, 1926.

Section 15. Inapplicability of the Act of State doctrine

Enforcement of arbitral agreements, confirmation of arbitral awards, and execution upon judgments based on orders confirming such awards shall not be refused on the basis of the Act of State doctrine.

Section 16. Appeals

a. An appeal may be taken from

1. an order—

A. refusing a stay of any action under section 3 of this title,

B. denying a petition under section 4 of this title to order arbitration to proceed,

C. denying an application under section 206 of this title to compel arbitration,

D. confirming or denying confirmation of an award or partial award, or

E. modifying, correcting, or vacating an award;

2. an interlocutory order granting, continuing, or modifying an injunction against an arbitration that is subject to this title; or

3. a final decision with respect to an arbitration that is subject to this title.

b. Except as otherwise provided in section 1292(b) of title 28, an appeal may not be taken from an interlocutory order—

1. granting a stay of any action under section 3 of this title;

2. directing arbitration to proceed under section 4 of this title;

3. compelling arbitration under section 206 of this title; or

4. refusing to enjoin an arbitration that is subject to this title.

Chapter 2. CONVENTION ON THE RECOGNITION AND ENFORCEMENT OF FOREIGN ARBITRAL AWARDS

Section 201. Enforcement of Convention

The Convention on the Recognition and Enforcement of Foreign Arbitral Awards of June 10, 1958, shall be enforced in United States courts in accordance with this chapter.

Section 202. Agreement or award falling under the Convention

An arbitration agreement or arbitral award arising out of a legal relationship, whether contractual or not, which is considered as commercial, including a transaction, contract, or agreement described in section 2 of this title, falls under the Convention. An agreement or award arising out of such a relationship which is entirely between citizens of the United States shall be deemed not to fall under the Convention unless that relationship involves property located abroad, envisages performance or enforcement abroad, or has some other reasonable relation with one or more foreign states. For the purpose of this section a corporation is a citizen of the United States if it is incorporated or has its principal place of business in the United States.

Section 203. Jurisdiction; amount in controversy

An action or proceeding falling under the Convention shall be deemed to arise under the laws and treaties of the United States. The district courts of the United States (including the courts enumerated in section 460 of title 28) shall have original jurisdiction over such an action or proceeding, regardless of the amount in controversy.

Section 204. Venue

An action or proceeding over which the district courts have jurisdiction pursuant to section 203 of this title may be brought in any such court in which save for the arbitration agreement an action or proceeding with respect to the controversy between the parties could be brought, or in such court for the district and division which embraces the place designated in the agreement as the place of arbitration if such place is within the United States.

Section 205. Removal of cases from State courts

Where the subject matter of an action or proceeding pending in a State court relates to an arbitration agreement or award falling under the Convention, the defendant or the defendants may, at any time before the trial thereof, remove such action or proceeding to the district court of the United States for the district and division embracing the place where the action or proceeding is pending. The procedure for removal of causes otherwise provided by law shall apply, except that the ground for removal provided in this section need not appear on the face of the complaint but may be shown in the petition for removal. For the purposes of Chapter 1 of this title any action or proceeding removed under this section shall be deemed to have been brought in the district court to which it is removed.

Section 206. Order to compel arbitration; appointment of arbitrators

A court having jurisdiction under this chapter may direct that arbitration be held in accordance with the agreement at any place therein provided for, whether that place is within or without the United States. Such court may also appoint arbitrators in accordance with the provisions of the agreement.

Section 207. Award of arbitrators; confirmation; jurisdiction; proceeding

Within three years after an arbitral award falling under the Convention is made, any party to the arbitration may apply to any court having jurisdiction under this chapter for an order confirming the award as against any other party to the arbitration. The court shall confirm the award unless it finds one of the grounds for refusal or deferral of recognition or enforcement of the award specified in the said Convention.

Section 208. Chapter 1; residual application

Chapter 1 applies to actions and proceedings brought under this chapter to the extent that chapter is not in conflict with this chapter or the Convention as ratified by the United States.

Chapter 3. INTER-AMERICAN CONVENTION ON INTERNATIONAL COMMERCIAL ARBITRATION

Section 301. Enforcement of Convention

The Inter-American Convention on International Commercial Arbitration of January 30, 1975, shall be enforced in United States courts in accordance with this chapter.

Section 302. Incorporation by reference

Sections 202, 203, 204, 205, and 207 of this title shall apply to this chapter as if specifically set forth herein, except that for the purposes of this chapter "the Convention" shall mean the Inter-American Convention.

Section 303. Order to compel arbitration; appointment of arbitrators; locale

(a) A court having jurisdiction under this chapter may direct that arbitration be held in accordance with the agreement at any place therein provided for, whether that place is within or without the United States. The court may also appoint arbitrators in accordance with the provisions of the agreement.

(b) In the event the agreement does not make provision for the place of arbitration or the appointment of arbitrators, the court shall direct that the arbitration shall be held and the arbitrators be appointed in accordance with Article 3 of the Inter-American Convention.

Section 304. Recognition and enforcement of foreign arbitral decisions and awards; reciprocity

Arbitral decisions or awards made in the territory of a foreign State shall, on the basis of reciprocity, be recognized and enforced under this chapter only if that State has ratified or acceded to the Inter-American Convention.

Section 305. Relationship between the Inter-American Convention and the Convention on the Recognition and Enforcement of Foreign Arbitral Awards of June 10, 1958

When the requirements for application of both the Inter-American Convention and the Convention on the Recognition and Enforcement of Foreign Arbitral Awards of June 10, 1958, are met, determination as to which Convention applies shall, unless otherwise expressly agreed, be made as follows:

1. If a majority of the parties to the arbitration agreement are citizens of a State or States that have ratified or acceded to the Inter-American Convention and are member States of the Organization of American States, the Inter-American Convention shall apply.

2. In all other cases the Convention on the Recognition and Enforcement of Foreign Arbitral Awards of June 10, 1958, shall apply.

Section 306. Applicable rules of Inter-American Commercial Arbitration Commission

a. For the purposes of this chapter the rules of procedure of the Inter-American Commercial Arbitration Commission referred to in Article 3 of the Inter-American Convention shall, subject to subsection (b) of this section, be those rules as promulgated by the Commission on July 1, 1988.

b. In the event the rules of procedure of the Inter-American Commercial Arbitration Commission are modified or amended in accordance with the procedures for amendment of the rules of that Commission, the Secretary of State, by regulation in accordance with section 553 of title 5, consistent with the aims and purposes of this Convention, may prescribe that such modifications or amendments shall be effective for purposes of this chapter.

Section 307. Chapter 1; residual application

Chapter 1 applies to actions and proceedings brought under this chapter to the extent chapter 1 is not in conflict with this chapter or the Inter-American Convention as ratified by the United States.

APPENDIX 8:
STATE AND FEDERAL STATUTES RELATING TO ARBITRATION ENFORCEMENT

JURISDICTION	STATUTE
United States	Federal Arbitration Act, 9 USC §§ 1 et seq.
United States	Administrative Dispute Resolution Act of 1996, 5 USC §§ 571 et seq.
Alabama	Code of Alabama, §§ 6-6-1 et seq.
Alaska	Alaska Statutes, §§ 09.43.010 et seq.
Arizona	Arizona Revised Statutes, §§12-1501 et seq.
Arkansas	Arkansas Statutes Annotated, §§ 16-108-101 et seq.
California	California Code of Civil Procedure, §§ 1280.2 et seq.
Colorado	Colorado Revised Statutes, §§ 13-22-201 et seq.
Connecticut	Connecticut General Statutes Annotated, §§ 52-408 et seq.
Delaware	Delaware Code Annotated, Title 10, §§ 5701 et seq.
District of Columbia	D.C.Code Annotated, Title 16, §§ 16-4301 et seq.
Florida	Florida Statutes Annotated, §§ 682.01 et seq.
Georgia	Code of Georgia, §§ 9-9-80 et seq.
Hawaii	Hawaii Revised Statutes, §§ 658-1 et seq.
Idaho	Idaho Code, §§ 7-901 et seq.
Illinois	Illinois Revised Statutes, Chapter 10, §§ 101 et seq.
Indiana	Indiana Code Annotated, §§ 34-4-1-1 et seq.

JURISDICTION	STATUTE
Iowa	Code of Iowa, §§ 679A et seq.
Kansas	Kansas Statutes, §§ 5-401 et seq.
Kentucky	Kentucky Revised Statutes, §§ 417.045 et seq.
Louisiana	Louisiana Revised Statutes, §§ 9:4201 et. seq.
Maine	Maine Revised Statutes Annotated, Title 14, §§ 5927 et seq.
Maryland	Maryland Courts & Judicial Procedure Code Annotated, §§ 3-201 et seq.
Massachusetts	Annotated Laws of Massachusetts, Chapter 251, §§ 1 et seq.
Michigan	Michigan Complied Laws, §§ 600.5001 et seq.
Minnesota	Minnesota Statutes, §§ 572.08 et seq.
Mississippi	Mississippi Code Annotated, §§ 11-15-1 et seq.
Missouri	Annotated Missouri Statutes, §§ 435.350 et seq.
Montana	Revised Montana Code Annotated, §§ 27-5-111 et seq.
Nebraska	Revised Statutes of Nebraska, §§ 25-260 et seq.
Nevada	Nevada Revised Statutes, §§ 38.015 et seq.
New Hampshire	New Hampshire Revised Statutes Annotated, §§ 542:1 et seq.
New Jersey	New Jersey Statutes Annotated, §§ 2A:24-1 et seq.
New Mexico	New Mexico Statutes Annotated, §§ 44-7-1 et seq.
New York	New York Civil Practice Law and Rules, §§ 7501 et seq.
North Carolina	General Statutes of North Carolina, §§ 1-567.1 et seq.
North Dakota	North Dakota Century Code, §§ 32-29.2-01 et seq.
Ohio	Ohio Revised Code Annotated, §§ 2711.01 et seq.
Oklahoma	Oklahoma Statutes Annotated, Title 15, §§ 801 et seq.
Oregon	Oregon Revised Statutes, §§ 33.210 et seq.
Pennsylvania	Pennsylvania Statutes Annotated, Title 42, §§ 7301 et seq.
Rhode Island	General Laws of Rhode Island, §§ 10-3-1 et seq.
South Carolina	Code of Laws of South Carolina, §§ 15-48-10 et seq.
South Dakota	South Dakota Codified Laws Annotated, §§ 21-25A-1 et seq.

JURISDICTION	STATUTE
Tennessee	Tennessee Code Annotated, §§ 29-5-301 et seq.
Texas	Texas Civ. Prac. & Rem, §§ 171.00 et seq.
Utah	Utah Code Annotated, §§ 78-319-1 et seq.
Vermont	Vermont Statutes Annotated, Title 12, §§ 5651 et seq.
Virginia	Code of Virginia Annotated, §§ 8.01-577 et seq.
Washington	Washington Revised Code Annotated, §§ 7.04.010 et seq.
West Virginia	West Virginia Code, §§ 55-10-1 et seq.
Wisconsin	Wisconsin Statutes Annotated, §§ 788.01 et seq.
Wyoming	Wyoming Statutes, §§ 1-36-101 et seq.

APPENDIX 9:
THE UNIFORM ARBITRATION ACT

**Act Relating to Arbitration and to Make Uniform the Law
With Reference Thereto**

Section 1: Validity of Arbitration Agreement

A written agreement to submit any existing controversy to arbitration or a provision in a written contract to submit to arbitration any controversy thereafter arising between the parties is valid, enforceable and irrevocable, save upon such grounds as exist at law or in equity for the revocation of any contract. This act also applies to arbitration agreements between employers and employees or between their respective representatives unless otherwise provided in the agreement.

Section 2: Proceedings to Compel or Stay Arbitration

(a) On application of a party showing an agreement described in Section 1, and the opposing party's refusal to arbitrate, the Court shall order the parties to proceed with arbitration, but if the opposing party denies the existence of the agreement to arbitrate, the Court shall proceed summarily to the determination of the issue so raised and shall order arbitration if found for the moving party, otherwise, the application shall be denied.

(b) On application, the courts may stay an arbitration proceeding commenced or threatened on a showing that there is no agreement to arbitrate. Such an issue, when in substantial and bona fide dispute, shall be forthwith and summarily tried and the stay ordered if found for the moving party. If found for the opposing party, the court shall order the parties to proceed to arbitration.

(c) If an issue referable to arbitration under the alleged agreement is involved in action or proceeding pending in a court having jurisdiction to hear applications under subdivision (a) of this Section, the application shall be made therein. Otherwise and subject to Section 18, the application may be made in any court of competent jurisdiction.

(d) Any action or proceeding involving an issue subject to arbitration shall be stayed if an order for arbitration or an application therefore has been made under this section or, if the issue is severable, the stay may be with respect thereto only. When the application is made in such action or proceeding, the order for arbitration shall include such stay.

(e) An order for arbitration shall not be refused on the ground that the claim in issue lacks merit or bona fides or because any fault or grounds for the claim sought to be arbitrated have not been shown.

Section 3: Appointment of Arbitrators by Courts

If the arbitration agreement provides a method of appointment of arbitrators, this method shall be followed. In the absence thereof, or if the agreed method fails or for any reason cannot be followed, or when an arbitrator appointed fails or is unable to act and his successor has not been duly appointed, the court on application of a party shall appoint one or more arbitrators. An arbitrator so appointed has all the powers of one specifically named in the agreement.

Section 4: Majority Action by Arbitrators

The powers of the arbitrators may be exercised by a majority unless otherwise provided by the agreement or by this act.

Section 5: Hearing

Unless otherwise provided by the agreement:

(a) The arbitrators shall appoint a time and place for the hearing and cause notification to the parties to be served personally or by registered mail not less than five days before the hearing. Appearance at the hearing waives such notice. The arbitrators may adjourn the hearing from time to time as necessary and, on request of a party and for good cause, or upon their own motion may postpone the hearing to a time not later than the date fixed by the agreement for marking the award unless the parties consent to a later date. The arbitrators may hear and determine the controversy upon the evidence produced notwithstanding the failure of a party duly notified to appear. The court on application may direct the arbitrators to proceed promptly with the hearing and determination of the controversy.

(b) The parties are entitled to be heard, to present evidence material to the controversy and to cross-examine witnesses appearing at the hearing.

(c) The hearing shall be conducted by all the arbitrators but a majority may determine any question and render a final award. If, during the course of the hearing, an arbitrator for any reason ceases to act, the remaining arbitrator or arbitrators appointed to act as neutrals may continue with the hearing and determination of the controversy.

Section 6: Representation by Attorney

A party has the right to be represented by an attorney at any proceeding or hearing under this act. A waiver thereof prior to the proceeding or hearing is ineffective.

Section 7: Witnesses, Subpoenas, Depositions

(a) The arbitrators may issue or cause to be issued subpoenas for the attendance of witnesses and for the production of books, records, documents and other evidence, and shall have the power to administer oaths. Subpoenas so issued shall be served, and upon application to the Court by a party or the arbitrators, enforced, in the manner provided by law for the service and enforcement of subpoenas in a civil action.

(b) On application of a party and for use as evidence, the arbitrators may permit a deposition to be taken, in the manner and upon the terms designated by the arbitrators, of a witness who cannot be subpoenaed or is unable to attend the hearing.

(c) All provisions of law compelling a person under subpoena to testify are applicable.

(d) Fees for attendance as a witness shall be the same as for a witness in Court.

Section 8: Award

(a) The award shall be in writing and signed by the arbitrators joining in the award. The arbitrators shall deliver a copy to each party personally or by registered mail, or as provided in this agreement.

(b) An award shall be made within the time fixed therefor by the agreement or, if not so fixed, within such time as the court orders on application of a party. The parties may extend the time in writing either before or after the expiration thereof. A party waives the objection that an award was not made within the time required unless he notifies the arbitrators of his objection prior to the delivery of the award to him.

Section 9: Change of Award by Arbitrators

On application of a party or, if an application to the court is pending under Sections 11, 12, or 13, on submission to the arbitrators by the court under such conditions as the court may order, the arbitrators may modify or correct the award upon the grounds stated in paragraphs (1) and (3) of subdivision (a) of Section 13, or for the purpose of clarifying the award. The application shall be made within twenty days after delivery of the award to the applicant. Written notice thereof shall be given forthwith to the opposing party, stating he must serve his objection thereto if any, within ten days from the notice. The award so modified or corrected is subject to the provisions of Sections 11, 12 and 13.

Section 10: Fees and Expenses of Arbitration

Unless otherwise provided in the agreement to arbitrate, the arbitrators' expenses and fees, together with other expenses, not including counsel fees, incurred in the conduct of the arbitration, shall be paid as provided in the award.

Section 11: Confirmation of an Award

(a) Upon application of a party, the court shall vacate an award where:

(1) The award was procured by corruption, fraud or other undue means;

(2) There was evident partiality by an arbitrator appointed as a neutral or corruption in any of the arbitrators or misconduct prejudicing the rights of any party;

(3) The arbitrators exceeded their powers;

(4) The arbitrators refused to postpone the hearing upon sufficient cause being shown therefor or refused to hear evidence material to the controversy or otherwise so conducted the hearing contrary to the provisions of Section 5, as to prejudice substantially the rights of a party; or

(5) There was no arbitration agreement and the issue was not adversely determined in proceedings under Section 2 and the party did not participate in the arbitration hearing without raising the objection;

But the fact that the relief was such that it could not or would not be granted by a court of law or equity is not ground for vacating or refusing to confirm the award.

(b) An application under this Section shall be made within ninety days after delivery of a copy of the award to the applicant, except that, if predicated upon corruption, fraud or other undue means, it shall be made within ninety days after such grounds are known or should have been known.

(c) In vacating the award on grounds other than stated in clause (5) of Subsection (a) the court may order a rehearing before new arbitrators chosen as provided in the agreement, or in the absence thereof, by the court in accordance with Section 3, or, if the award is vacated on grounds set forth in clauses (3), and (4) of Subsection (a) the court may order a rehearing before the arbitrators who made the award or their successors appointed in accordance with Section 3. The time within which the agreement requires the award to be made is applicable to the rehearing and commences from the date of the award.

(d) If the application to vacate is denied and no motion to modify or correct the award is pending, the court shall confirm the award.

Section 13: Modification or Correction of Award

(a) Upon application made within ninety days after delivery of a copy of the award to the applicant, the court shall modify or correct the award where:

(1) There was an evident miscalculation of figures or an evident mistake in the description of any person, thing or property referred to in the award;

(2) The arbitrators have awarded upon a matter not submitted to them and the award may be corrected without affecting the merits of the decision upon the issues submitted; or

(3) The award is imperfect in a matter of form, not affecting the merits of the controversy;

(b) If the application is granted, the court shall modify and correct the award so as to effects its intent and shall confirm the award as so modified and corrected. Otherwise, the court shall confirm the award as made.

(c) An application to modify or correct an award may be joined in the alternative with an application to vacate the award.

Section 14: Judgment or Decree on Award

Upon the granting of an order confirming, modifying or correcting an award, judgment or decree shall be entered in conformity therewith and be enforced as any other judgment or decree. Costs of the application and of the proceedings subsequent thereto, and disbursements may be awarded by the court.

Section 15: Judgment Roll, Docketing

(a) On entry of a judgment or decree, the clerk shall prepare the judgment roll consisting, to the extent filed, of the following:

(1) The agreement and each written extension of the time within which to make the award;

(2) The award;

(3) A copy of the order confirming, modifying or correcting the award; and

(4) A copy of the judgment or decree.

(b) The judgment or decree may be docketed as if rendered in an action.

Section 16: Applications to Court

Except as otherwise provided, an application to the court under this act shall be by motion and shall be heard in the manner and upon the notice provided by law or rule of court for the making and hearing of motions. Unless the parties have agreed otherwise, notice of an initial application for an order shall be served in the manner provided by law for the service of a summons and complaint.

Section 17: Court, Jurisdiction

The term "court" means any court of competent jurisdiction of this State. The making of an agreement described in Section 1 providing for arbitration in this State confers jurisdiction on the court to enforce the agreement under this act and to enter judgment on an award thereunder.

Section 18: Venue

An initial application shall be made to the court of the county in which the agreement provides the arbitration hearing shall be held or, if the hearing has been held, in the county in which it was held. Otherwise the application shall be made in the county where the adverse party resides or has a place of business or, if he has no residence or place of business in this State, to the court of any county. All subsequent applications shall be made to the court hearing the initial application unless the court otherwise directs.

Section 19: Appeals

(a) An appeal may be taken from:

(1) An order denying an application to compel arbitration under Section 2;

(2) An order granting an application to stay arbitration made under Section 2(b);

(3) An order confirming or denying confirmation of an award;

(4) An order modifying or correcting an award;

(5) An order vacating an award without directing a rehearing; or

(6) A judgment or decree entered pursuant to the provisions of this act.

(b) The appeal shall be taken in the manner and to the same extent as from orders or judgments in a civil action.

Section 20: Act Not Retroactive

This act applies only to agreements made subsequent to the taking effect of this act.

Section 21: Uniformity of Interpretation

This act shall be so construed as to effectuate its general purpose to make uniform the law of those states which enact it.

Section 22: Constitutionality

If any provision of this act or the application thereof to any person or circumstance is held invalid, the invalidity shall not affect other provisions or application of the act which can be given without the invalid provision or application, and to this end the provisions of the act are severable.

Section 23: Short Title

This act may be cited as the Uniform Arbitration Act.

Section 24: Repeal

All acts or parts of acts which are inconsistent with the provisions of this act are hereby repealed.

Section 25: Time of Taking Effect

This act shall take effect on [date].

APPENDIX 10:
SAMPLE CONTRACT ARBITRATION CLAUSE

Any controversy or claim arising out of or relating to this contract, or the breach thereof, shall be settled by arbitration administered by the American Arbitration Association in accordance with its Commercial Arbitration Rules, and judgment on the award rendered by the arbitrator(s) may be entered in any court having jurisdiction thereof.*

---

* Source: A Guide to Arbitration for Business People, American Arbitration Association, 1992.

APPENDIX 11:
DEMAND FOR ARBITRATION

Date:

To: (Name of the Party on Whom the Demand is Made)

Address:

Telephone:

Fax:

Name of Representative: (if known)

Name of Firm: (if Applicable)

Representative's Address:

Telephone:

Fax:

The named claimant, a party to an arbitration agreement contained in a written contract, dated _____ and providing for arbitration under the Voluntary Arbitration Rules of the American Arbitration Association, hereby demands arbitration thereunder. (Attach the arbitration clause or quote it hereunder.)

NATURE OF DISPUTE:

CLAIM OR RELIEF SOUGHT: (amount, if any):

HEARING LOCALE REQUESTED: (City and State)

You are hereby notified that copies of our arbitration agreement and this demand are being filed with the American Arbitration Association at its _____ office, with a request that it commence administration of the arbitration. Under the rules, you may file an answering statement within ten days after notice from the administrator.

Signed_____

Title: (may be signed by representative)

Name of Claimant:

Address: (to Be Used in Connection with this Case)

Telephone:

Fax:

Name of Representative

Representative's Address

Telephone:

Fax:

To institute proceedings, please send three copies of this demand and the arbitration agreement, with the filing fee as provided in the rules, to the AAA. Send the original demand to the respondent.*

---

*   Source: American Arbitration Association, 1999

APPENDIX 12:
SAMPLE AGREEMENT TO SUBMIT A
DISPUTE TO ARBITRATION

We, the undersigned parties, hereby agree to submit to arbitration administered by the American Arbitration Association under its Commercial Arbitration Rules the following controversy: [describe nature of dispute].

We further agree that the above controversy be submitted to three arbitrators.

We further agree that we will faithfully observe this agreement and the rules, and that we will abide by and perform any award rendered by the arbitrators and that a judgment of the court having jurisdiction may be entered on the award.*

---

* Source: A Guide to Arbitration for Business People, American Arbitration Association, 1992.

APPENDIX 13:
SUBMISSION TO DISPUTE RESOLUTION

The named parties hereby submit the following dispute for resolution under the applicable Rules of the American Arbitration Association.

Procedure Selected:

Binding Arbitration _____

Mediation Settlement _____

Other (Please describe)_____

THE NATURE OF THE DISPUTE

THE CLAIM OR RELIEF SOUGHT (the Amount, if Any):

TYPE OF BUSINESS:

Claimant _____

Respondent _____

PLACE OF HEARING:

We agree that, if binding arbitration is selected, we will abide by and perform any award rendered hereunder and that a judgement may be entered on the award.

To Be Completed by the Parties

Signed_____

Name of Party:

Address:

Telephone:

Fax:

Signed_____

Name of Party:

Address:

Telephone:

Fax:

Signed_____

Name of Representative of: (state which party)

Representative's Address

Telephone:

Fax:

Signed_____

Name of Representative of: (state which party)

Representative's Address

Telephone:

Fax:

Please file three copies with the AAA
If you have a question as to which rules apply, please contact the AAA.
Signatures of all parties are required for arbitration*.

---

*   Source: American Arbitration Association, 1999

APPENDIX 14:
COMMERCIAL ARBITRATION RULES OF THE AMERICAN ARBITRATION ASSOCIATION

1. Agreement of the Parties

The parties shall be deemed to have made these rules a part of their arbitration agreement whenever they have provided for arbitration by the American Arbitration Association (hereinafter AAA) or under its Commercial Arbitration Rules. These rules and any amendment of them shall apply in the form obtaining at the time the demand for arbitration or submission agreement is received by the AAA. The parties, by written agreement, may vary the procedures set forth in these rules.

2. Name of Tribunal

Any tribunal constituted by the parties for the settlement of their dispute under these rules shall be called the Commercial Arbitration Tribunal.

3. Administrator and Delegation of Duties

When parties agree to arbitrate under these rules, or when they provide for arbitration by the AAA and an arbitration is initiated under these rules, they thereby authorize the AAA to administer the arbitration. The authority and duties of the AAA are prescribed in the agreement of the parties and in these rules, and may be carried out through such of the AAA's representatives as it may direct.

4. National Panel of Arbitrators

The AAA shall establish and maintain a National Panel of Commercial Arbitrators and shall appoint arbitrators therefrom as hereinafter provided.

Regional Offices

The AAA may, in its discretion, assign the administration of an arbitration to any of its regional offices.

Initiation under an Arbitration Provision in a Contract

Arbitration under an arbitration provision in a contract shall be initiated in the following manner:

(a) The initiating party (hereinafter claimant) shall, within the time period, if any, specified in the contract(s), give written notice to the other party (hereinafter respondent) of its intention to arbitrate (demand), which notice shall contain a statement setting forth the nature of the dispute, the amount involved, if any, the remedy sought, and the hearing locale requested, and

(b) Shall file at any regional office of the AAA three copies of the notice and three copies of the arbitration provisions of the contract, together with the appropriate administrative fee as provided in the Administrative Fee Schedule.

The AAA shall give notice of such filing to the respondent or respondents. A respondent may file an answering statement in duplicate with the AAA within ten days after notice from the AAA, in which event the respondent shall at the same time send a copy of the answering statement to the claimant. If a counterclaim is asserted, it shall contain a statement setting forth the nature of the counterclaim, the amount involved, if any, and the remedy sought. If a counterclaim is made in the answering statement, the appropriate fee provided in the Administrative Fee Schedule shall be forwarded to the AAA with the answering statement. If no answering statement is filed within the stated time, it will be treated as a denial of the claim. Failure to file an answering statement shall not operate to delay the arbitration.

7. Initiation under a Submission

Parties to any existing dispute may commence an arbitration under these rules by filing at any regional office of the AAA three copies of a written submission to arbitrate under these rules, signed by the parties. It shall contain a statement of the mater in dispute, the amount of money involved, if any, the remedy sought, and the hearing locale requested, together with the appropriate administrative fee as provided in the Administrative Fee Schedule.

8. Changes of Claim

After filing of a claim, if either party desires to make any new or different claim or counterclaim, same shall be made in writing and filed with the AAA, and a copy shall be mailed to the other party, who shall have a period of ten days from the date of such mailing within which to file an answer with the AAA. After the arbitrator is appointed, however, no new or different claim may be submitted except with the arbitrator's consent.

9. Applicable Procedures

Unless the AAA in its discretion determines otherwise, the Expedited Procedures shall be applied in any case where no disclosed claim or counterclaim exceeds $50,000, exclusive of interest and arbitration costs. Parties may also agree to the Expedited Procedures in cases involving claims in excess of $50,000. The Expedited Procedures shall be applied as described in Sections 53 through 57 of these rules, in addition to any other portion of these rules that is not in conflict with the Expedited Procedures.

All other cases shall be administered in accordance with Sections 1 through 52 of these rules.

10. Administrative Conference, Preliminary Hearing, and Mediation Conference

At the request of any party or at the discretion of the AAA, an administrative conference with the AAA and the parties and/or their representatives will be scheduled in appropriate cases to expedite the arbitration proceedings.

In large or complex cases, at the request of any party or at the discretion of the arbitrator or the AAA, a preliminary hearing with the parties and/or their representatives and the arbitrator may be scheduled by the arbitrator to specify the issues to be resolved, to stipulate to uncontested facts, and to consider any other matters that will expedite the arbitration proceedings. Consistent with the expedited nature of arbitration, the arbitrator may, at the preliminary hearing, establish (i) the extent of and schedule for the production of relevant documents and other information, (ii) the identification of any witnesses to be called, and (iii) a schedule for further hearings to resolve the dispute.

With the consent of the parties, the AAA at any stage of the proceeding may arrange a mediation conference under the Commercial Mediation Rules, in order to facilitate settlement. The mediator shall not be an arbitrator appointed to the case. Where the parties to a pending arbitration agree to mediate under the AAA's rules, no additional administrative fee is required to initiate the mediation.

11. Fixing of Locale

The parties may mutually agree on the locale where the arbitration is to be held. If any party requests that the hearing be held in a specific locale and the other party files no objection thereto within ten days after notice of the request has been mailed to it by the AAA, the locale shall be the one requested. If a party objects to the locale requested by the other party, the AAA shall have the power to determine the locale and its decision shall be final and binding.

12. Qualifications of an Arbitrator

Any neutral arbitrator appointed pursuant to Section 13, 14, 15 or 54, or selected by mutual choice of the parties or their appointees, shall be subject to disqualification for the reasons specified in Section 19. If the parties specifically so agree in writing, the arbitrator shall not be subject to disqualification for those reasons.

Unless the parties agree otherwise, an arbitrator selected unilaterally by one party is a party-appointed arbitrator and is not subject to disqualification pursuant to Section 19.

The term "arbitrator" in these rules refers to the arbitration panel, whether composed of one or more arbitrators and whether the arbitrators are neutral or party appointed.

13. Appointment from Panel

If the parties have not appointed an arbitrator and have not provided any other method of appointment, the arbitrator shall be appointed in the following manner: immediately after the filing of the demand or submission, the AAA shall submit simultaneously to each party to the dispute an identical list of names of persons chosen from the panel.

Each party to the dispute shall have ten days from the mailing date in which to cross off any names objected to, number the remaining names in order of preference, and return the list to the AAA. If a party does not return the list within the time specified, all persons named therein shall be deemed acceptable. From among the persons who have been approved on both lists, and in accordance with the designated order of mutual preference, the AAA shall invite the acceptance of an arbitrator to serve. If the parties fail to agree on any of the persons named, or if acceptable arbitrators are unable to act, of if for any other reason the appointment cannot be made from the submitted lists, the AAA shall have the power to make the appointment from among other members of the panel without the submission of additional lists.

14. Direct Appointment by a Party

If the agreement of the parties names an arbitrator or specifies a method of appointing an arbitrator, that designation or method shall be followed. The notice of appointment, with the name and address of the arbitrator, shall be filed with the AAA by the appointing party. Upon the request of any appointing party, the AAA shall submit a list of members of the panel from which the party may, if it so desires, make the appointment.

If the agreement specifies a period of time within which an arbitrator shall be appointed and any party fails to make the appointment within that period, the AAA shall make the appointment.

If no period of time is specified in the agreement, the AAA shall notify the party to make the appointment. If within ten days thereafter an arbitrator has not been appointed by a party the AAA shall make the appointment.

15. Appointment of Neutral Arbitrator by Party-Appointed Arbitrators or Parties

If the parties have selected party-appointed arbitrators, of if such arbitrators have been appointed as provided in Section 14, and the parties have authorized them to appoint a neutral arbitrator within a specified time and no appointment is made within that time or any agreed extension thereof, the AAA may appoint a neutral arbitrator, who shall act as chairperson.

If no period of time is specified for appointment of the neutral arbitrator and the party-appointed arbitrators or the parties do not make the appointment within ten days from the date of appointment of the last party-appointed arbitrator, the AAA may appoint the neutral arbitrator, who shall act as chairperson.

If the parties have agreed that their party-appointed arbitrators shall appoint the neutral arbitrator from the panel, the AAA shall furnish to the party-appointed arbitrators, in the manner prescribed in Section 13, a list selected from the panel, and the appointment of the neutral arbitrator shall be made as prescribed in that section.

16. Nationality of Arbitrator in International Arbitration

Where the parties are nationals or residents of different countries, any neutral arbitrator shall, upon the request of either party, be appointed from among the nationals of a country other than that of any of the parties. The request must be made prior to the time set for the appointment of the arbitrator as agreed by the parties or set by these rules.

17. Number of Arbitrators

If the arbitration agreement does not specify the number of arbitrators, the dispute shall be heard and determined by one arbitrator, unless the AAA, in its discretion, directs that a greater number of arbitrators be appointed.

18. Notice to Arbitrator of Appointment

Notice of the appointment of the neutral arbitrator, whether appointed mutually by the parties or by the AAA, shall be mailed to the arbitrator by the AAA, together with a copy of these rules, and the signed acceptance of the arbitrator shall be filed with the AAA prior to the opening of the first hearing.

19. Disclosure and Challenge Procedure

Any person appointed as neutral arbitrator shall disclose to the AAA any circumstance likely to affect impartiality, including any bias or any financial or personal interest in the result of the arbitration or any past or present relationship with the parties or their representatives. Upon receipt of such information from the arbitrator or another source, the AAA shall communicate the information to the parties and, if it deems it appropriate to do so, to the arbitrator and others. Upon objection of a party to the continued service of a neutral arbitrator, the AAA shall determine whether the arbitrator should be disqualified and shall inform the parties of its decision, which shall be conclusive.

20. Vacancies

If for any reason an arbitrator is unable to perform the duties of the office, the AAA may, on proof satisfactory to it, declare the office vacant. Vacancies shall be filled in accordance with the applicable provisions of these rules.

In the event of a vacancy in a panel of neutral arbitrators after the hearings have commenced, the remaining arbitrator or arbitrators may continue with the hearing and determination of the controversy, unless the parties agree otherwise.

21. Date, Time and Place of Hearing

The arbitrator shall set the date, time and place for each hearing. The AAA shall mail to each party notice thereof at least ten days in advance, unless the parties by mutual agreement waive such notice or modify the terms thereof.

22. Representation

Any party may be represented by counsel or other authorized representative. A party intending to be so represented shall notify the other party and the AAA of the name and address of the representative at least three days prior to the date set for the hearing at which that person is first to appear. When such a representative initiates an arbitration or responds for a party, notice is deemed to have been given.

23. Stenographic Record

Any party desiring a stenographic record shall make arrangements directly with a stenographer and shall notify the other party of these arrangements in advance of the hearing. The requesting party or parties shall pay the cost of the record. If the transcript is agreed by the parties to be, or determined by the arbitrator to be, the official record of the proceeding, it must be made available to the arbitrator and to the other parties for inspection, at a date, time and place determined by the arbitrator.

24. Interpreters

Any party wishing an interpreter shall make all arrangements directly with the interpreter and shall assume the costs of the service.

25. Attendance at Hearings

The arbitrator shall maintain the privacy of the hearings unless the law provides to the contrary. Any person having a direct interest in the arbitration is entitled to attend hearings. The arbitrator shall otherwise have the power to require the exclusion of any witness, other than a party or other essential person, during the testimony of any other witness. It shall be discretionary with the arbitrator to determine the propriety of the attendance of any other person.

26. Postponements

The arbitrator for good cause shown may postpone any hearing upon the request of a party or upon the arbitrator's own initiative, and shall also grant such postponement when all of the parties agree thereto.

27. Oaths

Before proceeding with the first hearing, each arbitrator may take an oath of office and, if required by law, shall do so. The arbitrator may require witnesses to testify under oath administered by any duly qualified person and, if it is required by law or requested by any party, shall do so.

28. Majority Decision

All decisions of the arbitrators must be by majority. The award must also be made by a majority unless the concurrence of all is expressly required by the arbitration agreement or by law.

29. Order of Proceedings and Communication with Arbitrator

A hearing shall be opened by the filing of the oath of the arbitrator, where required; by the recording of the date, time and place of the hearing, and the presence of the arbitrator, the parties, and their representatives, if any; and by the receipt by the arbitrator of the statement of the claim and the answering statement, if any.

The arbitrator may, at the beginning of the hearing, ask for statements clarifying the issues involved. In some cases, part or all of the above will have been accomplished at the preliminary hearing conducted by the arbitrator pursuant to Section 10.

The complaining party shall then present evidence to support its claim. The defending party shall then present evidence supporting its defense. Witnesses for each party shall submit to questions or other examination. The arbitrator has the discretion to vary this procedure but shall afford a full and equal opportunity to all parties for the presentation of any material and relevant evidence.

Exhibits, when offered by either party, may be received in evidence by the arbitrator. The names and addresses of all witnesses and a description of the exhibits in the order received shall be made a pat of the record.

There shall be no direct communication between the parties and a neutral arbitrator other than at oral hearing, unless the parties and the arbitrator agree otherwise. Any other oral or written communication from the parties to the neutral arbitrator shall be directed to the AAA for transmittal to the arbitrator.

30. Arbitration in the Absence of a Party or Representative

Unless the law provides to the contrary, the arbitration may proceed in the absence of any party or representative who, after due notice, fails to be present or fails to obtain a postponement. An award shall not be made solely on the default of a party. The arbitrator shall require the party who is present to submit such evidence as the arbitrator may require for the making of an award.

31. Evidence

The parties may offer such evidence as is relevant and material to the dispute and shall produce such evidence as the arbitrator may deem necessary to an understanding and determination of the dispute. An arbitrator or other person authorized by law to subpoena witnesses or documents may do so upon the request of any party or independently.

The arbitrator shall be the judge of the relevance and materiality of the evidence offered, and conformity to legal rules of evidence shall be necessary. All evidence shall be take in the presence of all of the arbitrators and all of the parties, except where any of the parties is absent in default or has waived the right to be present.

32. Evidence by Affidavit and Post-hearing Filing of Documents or Other Evidence

The arbitrator may receive and consider the evidence of witnesses by affidavit, but shall give it only such weight as the arbitrator deems it entitled to after consideration of any objection made to its admission.

If the parties agree or the arbitrator directs that documents or other evidence be submitted to the arbitrator after the hearing, the documents or other evidence shall be filed with the AAA for transmission to the arbitrator. All parties shall be afforded an opportunity to examine such documents or other evidence.

33. Inspection or Investigation

An arbitrator finding it necessary to make an inspection or investigation in connection with the arbitration shall direct the AAA to so advise the parties. The arbitrator shall set the date and time and the AAA shall notify the parties. Any party who so desires may be present at such an inspection or investigation. In the event that one or all parties are not present at the inspection or investigation, the arbitrator shall make a verbal or written report to the parties and afford them an opportunity to comment.

34. Interim Measures

The arbitrator may issue such orders for interim relief as may be deemed necessary to safeguard the property that is the subject matter of the arbitration without prejudice to the rights of the parties or to the final determination of the dispute.

35. Closing of Hearing

The arbitrator shall specifically inquire of all parties whether they have any further proofs to offer or witnesses to be heard. Upon receiving negative replies or if satisfied that the record is complete, the arbitrator shall declare the hearing closed and a minute thereof shall be recorded. If briefs are to be filed, the hearings shall be declared closed as of the final date set by the arbitrator for the receipt of briefs. If documents are to be filed as provided in Section 32 and the date set for their receipt is later than that set for the receipt of briefs, the later date shall be the date of closing the hearing. The time limit within which the arbitrator is required to make the award shall commence to run, in the absence of other agreements by the parties upon the closing of the hearing.

36. Reopening of Hearing

The hearing may be reopened on the arbitrator's initiative, or upon application of a party, at any time before the award is made. If reopening the hearing would prevent the making of the award within the specific time agreed on by the parties in the contract(s) out of which the controversy has arisen, the matter may not be reopened unless the parties agree on an extension of time. When no specific date is fixed in the contract, the arbitrator may reopen the hearing and shall have thirty days from the closing of the reopened hearing within which to make the award.

37. Waiver of Oral Hearing

The parties may provide, by written agreement, for the waiver of oral hearings in any case. If the parties are unable to agree to the procedure, the AAA shall specify a fair and equitable procedure.

38. Waiver of Rules

Any party who proceeds with the arbitration after knowledge that any provision or requirement of these rules has not been complied with and who fails to state an objection thereto in writing shall be deemed to have waived the right to object.

39. Extension of Time

The parties may modify any period of time by mutual agreement. The AAA or the arbitrator may for good cause extend any period of time established by these rules, except the time for making the award. The AAA shall notify the parties of any extension.

40. Serving of Notice

Each party shall be deemed to have consented that any papers, notices, or process necessary or proper for the initiation or continuation of an arbitration under these rules; for any court action in connection therewith; or for the entry of judgment on any award made under these rules may be served on a party by mail addressed to the party or its representative at the last known address or by personal service, in or outside the state where the arbitration is to be held, provided that reasonable opportunity to be heard with regard thereto has been granted to the party.

The AAA and the parties may also use facsimile transmission, telex, telegram, or other written forms of electronic communication to give the notices required by these rules.

41. Time of Award

The award shall be made promptly by the arbitrator and, unless otherwise agreed by the parties or specified by law, no later than thirty days from the date of closing the hearing, or, if oral hearings have been waived, from the date of the AAA's transmittal of the final statements and proofs to the arbitrator.

42. Form of Award

The award shall be in writing and shall be signed by a majority of the arbitrators. It shall be executed in the manner required by law.

43. Scope of Award

The arbitrator may grant any remedy or relief that the arbitrator deems just and equitable and within the scope of the agreement of the parties, including, but not limited to, specified performance of a contract. The arbitrator shall, in the award, assess arbitration fees, expenses, and compensation as provided in Sections 48, 49 and 50 in favor of any party and, in the event that any administrative fees or expenses are due the AAA, in favor of the AAA.

44. Award Upon Settlement.

If the parties settle their dispute during the course of the arbitration, the arbitrator may set forth the terms of the agreed settlement in an award. Such an award is referred to as a consent award.

45. Delivery of Award to Parties

Parties shall accept as legal delivery of the award the placing of the award or a true copy thereof in the mail addressed to a party or its representative at the last known address, personal service of the award, or the filing of the award in any other manner that is permitted by law.

46. Release of Documents for Judicial Proceedings

The AAA shall, upon the written request of a party, furnish to the party, at its expense, certified copies of any papers in the AAA's possession that may be required in judicial proceedings relating to the arbitration.

47. Applications to Court and Exclusion of Liability

(a) No judicial proceeding by a party relating to the subject matter of the arbitration shall be deemed a waiver of the party's right to arbitrate.

(b) Neither the AAA nor any arbitrator in a proceeding under these rules is a necessary party in judicial proceedings relating to the arbitration.

(c) Parties to these rules shall be deemed to have consented that judgment upon the arbitration award may be entered in any federal or state court having jurisdiction thereof.

(d) Neither the AAA nor any arbitrator shall be liable to any party for any act or omission in connection with any arbitration conducted under these rules.

48. Administrative Fee

As a not-for-profit organization, the AAA shall prescribe an Administrative Fee Schedule and a Refund Schedule to compensate it for the cost of providing administrative services. The schedule in effect at the time the demand for arbitration or submission agreement is received shall be applicable.

The administrative fee shall be advanced by the initiating party or parties, subject to final apportionment by the arbitrator in the award.

When a claim or counterclaim is withdrawn or settled, the refund shall be made in accordance with the Refund Schedule.

The AAA may, in the event of extreme hardship on the part of any party, defer or reduce the administrative fee.

50. Neutral Arbitrator's Fee

Unless the parties agree otherwise, members of the National Panel of Commercial Arbitrators appointed as neutrals will serve without compensation for the first day of service.

Thereafter, compensation shall be based on the amount of service involved and the number of hearings. An appropriate daily rate and other arrangements will be discussed by the administrator with the parties and the arbitrator. If the parties fail to agree to the terms of compensation, an appropriate rate shall be established by the AAA and communicated in writing to the parties.

Any arrangement for the compensation of a neutral arbitrator shall be made through the AAA and not directly between the parties and the arbitrator. The terms of compensation of neutral arbitrators on a panel shall be identical.

Deposits

The AAA may require the parties to deposit in advance of any hearings such sums of money as it deems necessary to defray the expense of arbitration, including the arbitrator's fee, if any, and shall render an accounting to the parties and return any unexpended balance at the conclusion of the case.

Interpretation and Application of Rules

The arbitrator shall interpret and apply these rules insofar as they relate to the arbitrator's powers and duties. When there is more than one arbitrator and a difference arises among them concerning the meaning or application of these rules, it shall be decided by a majority vote. If that is unobtainable, either an arbitrator or a party may refer the question to the AAA for final decision. All other rules shall be interpreted and applied by the AAA.

Expedited Procedures

Notice by Telephone

The parties shall accept all notices from the AAA by telephone. Such notices by the AAA shall subsequently be confirmed in writing to the parties. Should there be a failure to confirm in writing any notice hereunder, the proceeding shall nonetheless be valid if notice has, in fact, been given by telephone.

54. Appointment and Qualifications of Arbitrator

Where no disclosed claim or counterclaim exceeds $50,000, exclusive of interest and arbitration costs, the AAA shall submit simultaneously to each party an identical list of five proposed arbitrators drawn from the National Panel of Commercial Arbitrators, from which one arbitrator shall be appointed.

Each party may strike two names from the list on a peremptory basis. The list is returnable to the AAA within seven days from the date of the AAA's mailing to the parties.

If for any reason the appointment of an arbitrator cannot be made from the list, the AAA may make the appointment from among other members of the panel without the submission of additional lists.

The parties will be given notice by telephone by the AAA of the appointment of the arbitrator, who shall be subject to disqualification for the reasons specified in Section 19. The parties shall notify the AAA, by telephone, within seven days of any objection to the arbitrator appointed. Any objection by a party to the arbitrator shall be confirmed in writing to the AAA with a copy to the other party or parties.

55. Date, Time and Place of Hearing

The arbitrator shall set the date, time, and place of the hearing. The AAA will notify the parties by telephone, at least seven days in advance of the hearing date. A formal Notice of Hearing will be sent by the AAA to the parties.

56. The Hearing

Generally, the hearing shall be completed within one day, unless the dispute is resolved by submission of documents under Section 37. The arbitrator, for good cause shown, may schedule an additional hearing to be held within seven days.

57. Time of Award

Unless otherwise agreed by the parties, the award shall be rendered not later than fourteen days from the date of the closing of the hearing.*

---

*   Source: American Arbitration Association, Commercial Arbitration Rules of the American Arbitration Association: As Amended and in Effect January 1, 1991.

APPENDIX 15:
SAMPLE CONTRACT MEDIATION CLAUSE

If a dispute arises out of or relates to this contract, or the breach thereof, and if said dispute cannot be settled through negotiation, the parties agree first to try in good faith to settle the dispute by mediation administered by the American Arbitration Association under its Commercial Mediation Rules, before resorting to arbitration, litigation, or some other dispute resolution procedure.*

---

*   Source: American Arbitration Association, 1993.

APPENDIX 16:
REQUEST FOR MEDIATION

Date: To: (Name of the Party on Whom the Demand is Made)

Address:

Telephone:

Fax:

The undersigned party to an agreement contained in a written contract dated _____, providing for mediation under the Mediation Rules of the American Arbitration Association, hereby requests mediation thereunder. (Attach the mediation clause or quote it hereunder.)

NATURE OF DISPUTE:

THE CLAIM OR RELIEF SOUGHT: (the amount, if any)

TYPE OF BUSINESS:

    Filing Party _____

    Responding Party _____

MEDIATION LOCALE REQUESTED:

You are hereby notified that copies of our mediation agreement and of this request are being filed with the American Arbitration Association office, with the request that it commence the administration of the mediation.

Signed_____

Title: (may be signed by representative)

Name of Filing Party:

Address: (to Be Used in Connection with this Case)

Telephone:

Fax:

Name of Representative

Representative's Address

Telephone:

Fax:

To institute proceedings, please send three copies of this request with the administrative fee, as provided for in the rules, to the AAA. Send the original request to the responding party.

If you have a question as to which rules apply, please contact the AAA. *

---

*   Source: American Arbitration Association, 1999

APPENDIX 17:
SAMPLE AGREEMENT TO SUBMIT A
DISPUTE TO MEDIATION

The parties hereby submit the following dispute to mediation administered by the American Arbitration Association under its Commercial Mediation rules. (may also detail the qualifications of the mediator(s), method of payment, locale of meetings and any other item of concern to the parties).*

---

*   Source: American Arbitration Association, 1993.

APPENDIX 18:
SETTLEMENT AGREEMENT AND MUTUAL
GENERAL RELEASE OF CLAIMS

AGREEMENT made as of the ____ day of January 2000, between JOHN DOE, Post Office Box 1000, Smalltown, USA 54321 (hereinafter "Doe") and JAMES SMITH, doing business as FRIENDLY GROCERS, located at 123 Main Street, Smalltown, USA 54321, (hereinafter, "Friendly").

IN CONSIDERATION of the mutual covenants and agreements herein contained, the parties hereto agree as follows:

1. In full, final and complete settlement of any and all claims, as provided herein below, and upon execution of this Agreement by the parties, Friendly agrees to pay Doe the total sum of Five Thousand ($5,000) Dollars by check, subject to collection.

2. Doe hereby releases and forever discharges the Friendly, its affiliated organizations, and its officers, directors, trustees, employees, agents, attorneys, successors and heirs, from any and all claims arising out of or in connection with any acts or omissions by Friendly.

3. Specifically, Doe releases Friendly from any and all claims resulting from physical injuries sustained as a result of a slip and fall on Friendly's premises.

4. The parties agree to keep the terms of this settlement, and the allegations giving rise to this Agreement, completely confidential, and will not hereinafter disclose any information concerning them to anyone, including any newspaper, magazine, radio or television station, or any other media, or any agents, employees or representatives of such media.

5. This Agreement shall be binding upon, and inure to the benefit of, each of the parties to this Agreement, and upon their respective heirs, administrators, representatives, executors and successors, if any.

6. This Agreement constitutes the entire agreement between the parties hereto and supersedes any and all other agreements, understandings, negotiations, or discussions, either oral or in writing, express or implied between the parties hereto.

7. This Agreement may not be amended, altered, modified or otherwise changed, except in a writing executed by the parties hereto.

IN WITNESS WHEREOF, the parties hereto have caused this agreement to be executed as of the date above set forth.

DATED:

BY:_____

JOHN DOE

BY:_____

JAMES SMITH d/b/a FRIENDLY GROCERS

VERIFICATION

STATE OF   )

        : ss.:

COUNTY OF)

On the _____ day of _____, 2000, before me personally came JOHN DOE, to me known to be the individual described in and who executed the foregoing instrument, and acknowledged that he executed the same.

_____

JOHN DOE

STATE OF   )

        : ss.:

COUNTY OF   )

On the _____ day of _____, 2000, before me personally came JAMES SMITH, to me known to be the individual described in and who executed the foregoing instrument, and acknowledged that he executed the same.

_____

JAMES SMITH

APPENDIX 19:
CORPORATE POLICY STATEMENT ON ALTERNATIVE DISPUTE RESOLUTION

COMPANY NAME:_____

We recognize that for many business disputes there is a less expensive, more effective method of resolution than the traditional lawsuit. Alternative dispute resolution (ADR) procedures involve collaborative techniques that can often spare businesses the high cost and wear and tear of litigation.

In recognition of the foregoing, we subscribe to the following statement of principle on behalf of our company and its domestic subsidiaries listed below. In the event of a business dispute between our company and another company that has made or will then make a similar statement, we are prepared to explore with that other party resolution of the dispute through negotiation or ADR techniques before pursuing full-scale litigation. If either party believes that the dispute is not suitable for ADR techniques, or if such techniques do not produce results satisfactory to the disputant, either party may proceed with litigation.

List of domestic operating subsidiaries:

_____

_____

_____

Chief Executive Officer

By: _____

Chief Executive Officer

By: _____

Chief Legal Officer

Dated:_____ *

---

* Source: Center for Public Resources (CPR) Legal Program, Containing Legal Costs: ADR Strategies for Corporations, Law Firms and Government; New York, NY: Center for Public Resources, 1988.

APPENDIX 20:
AAA ARBITRATION REQUEST FORM
UNDER THE NEW YORK STATE MOTOR
VEHICLE NO-FAULT INSURANCE LAW

 American Arbitration Association
Dispute Resolution Services Worldwide

NEW YORK MOTOR VEHICLE NO-FAULT INSURANCE LAW
ARBITRATION REQUEST FORM

(FOR PERSONAL INJURIES SUSTAINED ON AND AFTER 12/1/77)

OPTIONAL NO-FAULT ARBITRATION IS FINAL AND BINDING EXCEPT FOR THE LIMITED
GROUNDS FOR REVIEW SET FORTH IN THE LAW AND REGULATIONS. UPON RECEIPT
OF THIS REQUEST, THE AMERICAN ARBITRATION ASSOCIATION WILL ATTEMPT TO
RESOLVE THE DISPUTE. IF THE DISPUTE CANNOT BE RESOLVED, YOUR CASE WILL
BE FORWARDED FOR ARBITRATION. IF YOU WISH TO ARBITRATE YOUR CLAIM
COMPLETE BOTH SIDES OF THIS FORM TO THE BEST OF YOUR ABILITY. PLEASE
PRINT OR TYPE.

APPLICANT FOR BENEFITS			AS ASSIGNEE
			___ YES
LAST NAME	FIRST NAME	ADDRESS	___ NO
INJURED PERSON			DATE OF ACCIDENT
LAST NAME	FIRST NAME	ADDRESS	
POLICYHOLDER			POLICY NUMBER
LAST NAME	FIRST NAME	ADDRESS	
INSURER OR SELF-INSURER		INSURER'S CLAIMS OFFICE ADDRESS	
INSURER'S REPRESENTATIVE		TELEPHONE NUMBER	CLAIM OR FILE NUMBER

ACCIDENT LOCATION _____

DESCRIPTION OF ACCIDENT _____

WAS INSURER CONTACTED AFTER CLAIM WAS SUBMITTED?_____

NAME AND TITLE OF PERSON CONTACTED _____

DATE OF LAST CONTACT _____

REASON GIVEN BY INSURER FOR NONPAYMENT OF CLAIM(S) DETAILED ON REVERSE SIDE:_____

REASON YOU BELIEVE THE DENIED OR OVERDUE BENEFITS SHOULD BE PAID_____

SUPPLY DETAILS OF DISPUTE ON REVERSE SIDE

AAA FORM AR-12/99

DETAILS OF DISPUTED CLAIM

_____Loss of Earnings: Date claim made:_____   Gross earnings per month:$ _____

Period in dispute: From: _____ To: _____   Amount claimed: $_____

_____Medical (Attach bills in dispute):

DOCTOR, HOSPITAL OR OTHER HEALTH PROVIDER	AMOUNT OF EACH BILL	AMOUNT PAID	UNPAID OR DISPUTED BALANCE	DATES OF SERVICE	DATE BILL MAILED	WAS VERIFICATION REQUESTED		
						NO	YES	DATE SUPPLIED

_____Other Necessary Expense(s) (Attach bills in dispute):

TYPE OF EXPENSE CLAIMED	AMOUNT CLAIMED	DATE INCURRED	DATE MAILED	AMOUNT IN DISPUTE

____DEATH BENEFIT: DATE DEATH CERTIFICATE MAILED TO INSURER:_____

___INTEREST

BENEFIT PAID LATE	AMOUNT OF BILL	DATE MAILED TO INSURER	WAS VERIFICATION REQUESTED?			DATE PAID BY INSURER
			NO	YES	SUPPLIED DATE	

___ATTORNEY'S FEE

ANY PERSON WHO KNOWINGLY AND WITH INTENT TO DEFRAUD ANY INSURANCE COMPANY OR OTHER PERSON FILES AN APPLICATION FOR INSURANCE OR STATEMENT OF CLAIM CONTAINING ANY MATERIALLY FALSE INFORMATION, OR CONCEALS FOR THE PURPOSE OF MISLEADING, INFORMATION CONCERNING ANY FACT MATERIAL THERETO, COMMITS A FRAUDULENT INSURANCE ACT, WHICH IS A CRIME, AND SHALL ALSO BE SUBJECT TO A CIVIL PENALTY NOT TO EXCEED FIVE THOUSAND DOLLARS AND THE STATED VALUE OF THE CLAIM FOR EACH SUCH VIOLATION.

THIS FORM IS SUBSCRIBED AND AFFIRMED
BY THE APPLICANT AS TRUE UNDER THE PENALTY OF PERJURY
THE APPLICANT AFFIRMS THAT A COPY OF THIS COMPLETED FORM HAS BEEN MAILED
TO THE INSURER AGAINST WHOM ARBITRATION IS BEING REQUESTED

ARBITRATION REQUESTED BY:	NAME OF LAW FIRM, IF ANY
LAST NAME FIRST NAME	
TELEPHONE NUMBER	ADDRESS
SIGNATURE	ARE YOU AN ATTORNEY? ___YES ___NO	DATE

HOW TO FILE

1. MAIL THIS COMPLETED FORM AND ALL REQUESTED ATTACHMENTS IN DUPLICATE TOGETHER WITH A $40.00 FILING FEE PAYABLE TO THE AMERICAN ARBITRATION ASSOCIATION TO:

AMERICAN ARBITRATION ASSOCIATION
NEW YORK NO-FAULT CONCILIATION CENTER
65 BROADWAY
NEW YORK, NEW YORK 10006

2. MAIL A COPY OF THIS FORM TO THE INSURER AGAINST WHOM YOU ARE REQUESTING ARBITRATION AND RETAIN A COPY FOR YOUR RECORDS.

AAA FORM AR-12/99

GLOSSARY

American Arbitration Association (AAA)	National organization of arbitrators from whose panel arbitrators are selected for labor and civil disputes.
Answer	In a civil proceeding, the principal pleading on the part of the defendant in response to the plaintiff's complaint.
Appeal	Resort to a higher court for the purpose of obtaining a review of a lower court decision.
Appellate Court	A court having jurisdiction to review the law as applied to a prior determination of the same case.
Arbitration	The reference of a dispute to an impartial person chosen by the parties to the dispute who agree in advance to abide by the arbitrator's award issued after a hearing at which both parties have an opportunity to be heard.
Arbitration Acts	Federal and state laws which provide for submission of disputes to the process of arbitration.
Arbitration and Award	An affirmative defense to the effect that the subject matter of the action has been settled by a prior arbitration.

Arbitration Board	A panel of arbitrators appointed to hear and decide a dispute according to the rules of arbitration.
Arbitration Clause	A clause inserted in a contract providing for compulsory arbitration in case of dispute as to the rights or liabilities under such contract.
Arbitrator	A private, disinterested person, chosen by the parties to a disputed question, for the purpose of hearing their contention, and giving judgment between them.
Award	The final and binding decision of an arbitrator, made in writing and enforceable in court under state and federal statutes.
Case Administrator	Employees of the American Arbitration Association who are assigned to administer cases. The case administrator is responsible for the general management of a particular case, including panel selection, scheduling and exchange of information among the parties.
Caucuses	Meetings in which a mediator talks with the parties individually to discuss the issues.
Claimants	The parties who bring the arbitration petition, also known as plaintiffs.
Collective Bargaining	A procedure looking toward making of collective agreements between an employer and an accredited representative of employees concerning wages, hours, and other conditions of employment. Collective bargaining requires that the parties deal with each other with open and fair minds and contemplates the stabilization of employment relations to enable free flow of commerce.
Collective Bargaining Agreement	An Agreement between an employer and a labor union which regulates terms and conditions of employment.

Complaint	In a civil proceeding, the first pleading of the plaintiff setting out the facts on which the claim for relief is based.
Compromise and Settlement	An arrangement arrived at, either in court or out of court, for settling a dispute upon what appears to the parties to be equitable terms.
Compulsory Arbitration	Arbitration which occurs when the consent of one of the parties is enforced by statutory provisions.
Conciliation	Conciliation is often used interchangeably with mediation to describe a method of dispute settlement whereby parties clarify issues and narrow differences through the aid of a neutral facilitator.
Counterclaims	Counterdemands made by a respondent in his or her favor against a claimant. They are not mere answers or denials of the claimant's allegation.
Court of Conciliation	A court which proposes terms of adjustment of a dispute so as to avoid litigation.
Defendant	In a civil proceeding, the party responding to the complaint.
Demand for Arbitration	A unilateral filing of a claim in arbitration based on the filer's contractual or statutory right to do so.
Deposition	A method of pretrial discovery which consists of a statement of a witness under oath, taken in question and answer form as it would be in court, with opportunity given to the adversary to be present and cross-examine, with all being reported and transcribed stenographically.
Discovery	Modern pretrial procedure by which one party gains information held by another party.

Fact-Finder In a judicial or administrative proceeding, the person, or group of persons, that has the responsibility of determining the acts relevant to decide a controversy. It is the role of a jury in a jury trial. In a non-jury trial, the judge sits both as a fact-finder and as the trier of law.

Fact Finding A process by which parties present their evidence and make their arguments to a neutral person who issues a nonbinding report based on the findings which usually contains a recommendation for settlement.

Hearing A proceeding during which evidence is taken for the purpose of determining the facts of a dispute and reaching a decision.

Jurisdiction The power to hear and determine a case.

Mediation The act of a third person in intermediating between two contending parties with a view to persuading them to adjust or settle their dispute but without the authority to make a binding decision.

Mediation/ Arbitration (Med/Arb) Combination of mediation and arbitration which utilizes a neutral selected to serve as both mediator and arbitrator in a dispute. The techniques of persuasion and discussion, as used in mediation, are combined with the arbitrator's authority to issues a final and binding decision, when necessary.

Mediation and Conciliation Service An independent department of the federal government charged with trying to settle labor disputes by conciliation and mediation.

Mediator One who interposes between parties at variance for the purpose of reconciling them.

Minitrial	A confidential, nonbinding exchange of information, intended to facilitate settlement. The goal of a minitrial is to encourage prompt, cost-effective resolution of complex litigation. Minitrial seeks to narrow the areas of controversy, dispose of collateral issues, and encourage a fair and equitable settlement.
Motion	An application to the court requesting an order or ruling in favor of the applicant.
National Labor Relations Act	A federal statute known as the Wagner Act of 1935 and amended by the Taft-Hartley Act of 1947, which established the National Labor Relations Board which is charged with regulating the relations between employers and employees.
National Labor Relations Board	An independent agency created by the National Labor Relations Act of 1935 (Wagner Act), as amended by the acts of 1947 (Taft-Hartley Act) and 1959 (Landrum-Griffin Act). The two principal functions of the Board pursuant to the Act are (1) to prevent and remedy unfair labor practices by employers and labor organizations or their agents; and (2) conducting secret ballot elections among employees in appropriate collective bargaining units to determine whether or not they desire to be represented by a labor organization.
National Mediation Board	Organization created by an act of Congress on June 21, 1934 amending the Railway Labor Act, for the purposes of (1) mediating disputes over wages, hours and working conditions which arise between rail and air carriers and organizations representing their employees, and (2) investigating representation disputes and certifying of employee organizations as representatives of crafts or classes of carrier employees.
Negotiation	The process in which the parties to a dispute communicate their differences to each other, through conference, discussion and compromise, in an attempt to resolve them.

No-Fault Divorce	A divorce which is granted without the necessity of finding a spouse to have been guilty of some marital misconduct.
Original Jurisdiction	The jurisdiction of a court to hear a matter in the first instance.
Parties	The disputants.
Partnering	An alternative method of dispute resolution used in the construction industry. Partnering is a long-term commitment between two or more organizations for the purpose of achieving their specific business objectives by maximizing the effectiveness of each participant's resources.
Petitioner	One who presents a petition to a court or other body either in order to institute an equity proceeding or to take an appeal from a judgment.
Plaintiff	In a civil proceeding, the one who initially brings the lawsuit.
Precedent	A previously decided case which is recognized as authority for the disposition of future cases.
Respondent	The responding party, also known as the defendant.
Statute of Limitations	Any law which fixes the time within which parties must take judicial action to enforce rights or else be thereafter barred from enforcing them.
Submission	The filing of a dispute to a dispute resolution process.
Summary Jury Trial	Summary presentations by counsel in complex cases before a jury impaneled to make findings which are advisory, absent the agreement of the parties otherwise.

Summons A mandate requiring the appearance of the defendant in an action under penalty of having judgment entered against him for failure to do so.

Transcript An official and certified copy of what transpired in court or at an out-of-court deposition.

Trial A judicial examination of issues between parties, whether they are issues of law or of fact, before a court that has jurisdiction over the cause.

Voluntary Arbitration Arbitration which occurs by mutual and free consent of the parties.

BIBLIOGRAPHY

A Guide to Arbitration for Business People. American Arbitration Association, 1992.

American Arbitration Association (Date Visited: June 2000) [http:www.adr.org].

Black's Law Dictionary, Fifth Edition. St. Paul, MN: West Publishing Company, 1979.

Bluestone, Barry and Bluestone, Irving Negotiating the Future: A Labor Perspective on American Business. New York, NY: BasicBooks, A Division of Harper Collins Publishers, Inc., 1992.

Coulson, Robert Business Arbitration: What You Need to Know, Fourth Edition. New York, NY: American Arbitration Association, 1991.

Coulson, Robert How to Stay Out of Court. New York, NY: American Arbitration Association, 1984.

CPR Legal Program Containing Legal Costs: ADR Strategies for Corporations, Law Firms and Government. New York, NY: Center For Public Resources, 1988.

Craver, Charles B. Effective Legal Negotiation and Settlement. Charlottesville, VA: The Michie Company, 1993.

Crowley, Thomas E. Settle It Out of Court: How to Resolve Business and Personal Disputes Using Mediation, Arbitration and Negotiation. New York, NY: John Wiley & Sons, Inc., 1994.

Dispute Resolution Program Directory. Washington, DC: American Bar Association, 1990.

Family Dispute Resolution. Washington, DC: American Bar Association, 1990.

Gifis, Steven H. Barron's Law Dictionary, Second Edition. Woodbury, NY: Barron's Educational Series, Inc., 1984.

Hill, Marvin F. and Sincropi, Anthony V. Remedies in Arbitration. Washington, DC: Bureau of National Affairs, Inc., 1991.

Leeson, Susan M. and Johnston, Bryan M. Ending It: Dispute Resolution in America. Cincinnati, OH: Anderson Publishing Co., 1988.

Lynch, Hon. Eugene F., Reed, Barry C., Young, Douglas R., Taylor, Stephen E., Purver, Jonathan M., Davis III, James J. Negotiation and Settlement. Rochester, NY: Lawyers Cooperative Publishing, 1992.

Moore, Christopher W. The Mediation Process: Practical Strategies for Resolving Conflict. San Francisco, CA: Jossey-Bass Publishers, 1986.

Neuman, Diane Divorce Mediation: How to Cut the Cost & Stress of Divorce. New York, NY: Henry Holt and Company, Inc., 1989.

New York's New Car Lemon Law: A Guide for Consumers. New York State Department of Law, 1990.

New York's Used Car Lemon Law: A Guide for Consumers. New York State Department of Law, 1991.

Singer, Linda R. Settling Disputes. Boulder, CO: Westview Press, 1990.

Steiner, Julius M. The Arbitration Handbook. New York, NY: Executive Enterprises, Inc., 1989.